The Lay of the Land

The Lay of the Land

Dallas Lore Sharp

With Drawings By
R. Bruce Horsfall

LIVING BOOK
PRESS

This edition published 2019
By Living Book Press

Copyright © Living Book Press, 2019

Originally published in 1908

ISBN: 978-1-925729-88-7

NATIONAL LIBRARY OF AUSTRALIA

A catalogue record for this book is available from the National Library of Australia

Contents

I

The Muskrats are Building

WE have had a series of long, heavy rains, and water is standing over the swampy meadow. It is a dreary stretch, this wet, sedgy land in the cold twilight, drearier than any part of the woods or the upland pastures. They are empty, but the meadow is flat and wet, naked and all unsheltered. And a November night is falling.

The darkness deepens. A raw wind is rising. At nine o'clock the moon swings round and full to the crest of the ridge, and pours softly over. I button the heavy ulster close, and in my rubber boots go down to the river and follow it out to the middle of the meadow, where it meets the main ditch at the sharp turn toward the swamp. Here at the bend, behind a clump of black alders, I sit quietly down and wait.

I am not mad, nor melancholy; I am not after copy. Nothing is the matter with me. I have come out to the bend to watch the muskrats building, for that small mound up the ditch is not an old haycock, but a half-finished muskrat house.

The moon climbs higher. The water on the meadow shivers in the light. The wind bites through my heavy coat and

1

sends me back, but not until I have seen one, two, three little figures scaling the walls of the house with loads of mud-and-reed mortar. I am driven back by the cold, but not until I know that here in the desolate meadow is being rounded off a lodge, thick-walled and warm, and proof against the longest, bitterest of winters.

This is near the end of November. My wood is in the cellar; I am about ready to put on the double windows and storm doors; and the muskrats' house is all but finished. Winter is at hand: but we are prepared, the muskrats even better prepared than I, for theirs is an adequate house, planned perfectly.

Throughout the summer they had no house, only their tunnels into the sides of the ditch, their roadways out into the grass, and their beds under the tussocks or among the roots of the old stumps. All these months the water had been low in the ditch, and the beds among the tussocks had been safe and dry enough.

Now the autumnal rains have filled river and ditch, flooded the tunnels, and crept up into the beds under the tussocks. Even a muskrat will creep out of his bed when cold, wet water creeps in. What shall he do for a house? He does not want to leave his meadow. The only thing to do is to build,—move from under the tussock, out upon the top, and here, in the deep, wiry grass, make a new bed, high and dry above the rising water, and close the new bed in with walls that circle and dome and defy the winter.

Such a house will require a great deal of work to build. Why not combine, make it big enough to hold half a dozen, save labor and warmth, and, withal, live sociably together? So they left, each one his bed, and joining efforts, started, about the middle of October, to build this winter house.

Slowly, night after night, the domed walls have been rising, although for several nights at a time there would be no apparent progress with the work. The builders were in no hurry, it seems; the cold was far off; but it is coming, and to-night it feels near and keen. And to-night there is no loafing about the lodge.

When this house is done, then the rains may descend, and the floods come, but it will not fall. It is built upon a tussock; and a tussock, you will know, who have ever grubbed at one, has hold on the bottom of creation. The winter may descend, and the boys, and foxes, come,—and they will come, but not before the walls are frozen,—yet the house stands. It is boy-proof, almost; it is entirely rain-, cold-, and fox-proof. Many a time I have hacked at its walls with my axe when fishing through the ice, but I never got in. I have often seen, too, where the fox has gone round and round the house in the snow, and where, at places, he has attempted to dig into the frozen mortar; but it was a foot thick, as hard as flint, and utterly impossible for his pick and shovel.

Yet strangely enough the house sometimes fails of the very purpose for which it was erected. I said the floods may come. So they may, ordinarily; but along in March when one comes as a freshet, it rises sometimes to the dome of the house, filling the single bedchamber and drowning the dwellers out. I remember a freshet once in the end of February that flooded Lupton's Pond and drove the muskrats of the whole pond village to their ridgepoles, to the bushes, and to whatever wreckage the waters brought along.

The best laid schemes o' *muskrats too*
Gang aft a-gley.

But ganging a-gley is not the interesting thing, not the point with my muskrats: it is rather that my muskrats, and the mice that Burns ploughed up, the birds and the bees, and even the very trees of the forest, have foresight. They all look ahead and provide against the coming cold. That a mouse, or a muskrat, or even a bee, should occasionally prove foresight to be vain, only shows that the life of the fields is very human. Such foresight, however, oftener proves entirely adequate for the winter, dire as some of the emergencies are sure to be.

> The north wind doth blow,
> And we shall have snow,
> And what will Robin do then,
> Poor thing?

And what will Muskrat do? and Chipmunk? and Whitefoot? and little Chickadee? poor things! Never fear. Robin has heard the trumpets of the north wind and is retreating leisurely toward the south, wise thing! Muskrat is building a warm winter lodge; Chipmunk has already dug his but and ben, and so far down under the stone wall that a month of zeros could not break in; Whitefoot, the woodmouse, has stored the hollow poplar stub full of acorns, and has turned Robin's deserted nest, near by, into a cosy house; and Chickadee, dear thing, Nature herself looks after him. There are plenty of provisions for the hunting, and a big piece of suet on my lilac bush. His clothes are warm, and he will hide his head under his wing in the elm-tree hole when the north wind doth blow, and never mind the weather.

I shall not mind it either, not so much, anyway, on account of Chickadee. He lends me a deal of support. So do Chipmunk, Whitefoot, and Muskrat.

This lodge of my muskrats in the meadow makes a difference, I am sure, of at least ten degrees in the mean temperature of my winter. How can the out-of-doors freeze entirely up with such a house as this at the middle of it? For in this house is life, warm life,—and fire. On the coldest day I can look out over the bleak white waste to where the house shows, a tiny mound in the snow, and I can see the fire burn, just as I can see and feel the glow when I watch the slender blue wraith rise into the still air from the chimney of the old farmhouse along the road below. For I share in the life of both houses; and not less in the life of the mud house of the meadow, because, instead of Swedes, they are muskrats who live there. I can share the existence of a muskrat? Easily. I like to curl up with the three or four of them in that mud house and there spend the worst days of the winter. My own big house here on the hilltop is sometimes cold. And the wind! If sometimes I could only drive the insistent winter wind from the house corners! But down in the meadow the house has no corners; the mud walls are thick, so thick and round that the shrieking wind sweeps past unheard, and all unheeded the cold creeps over and over the thatch, then crawls back and stiffens upon the meadow.

The doors of our house in the meadow swing open the winter through. Just outside the doors stand our stacks of fresh calamus roots, and iris, and arum. The roof of the universe has settled close and hard upon us,—a sheet of ice extending from the ridge of the house far out to the shores of the meadow. The winter is all above the roof—outside. It blows and snows and freezes out there. In here, beneath the ice-roof, the roots of the sedges are pink and tender; our roads are all open and they run every way, over all the rich, rooty meadow.

The muskrats are building. Winter is coming. The muskrats are making preparations, but not they alone. The preparation for hard weather is to be seen everywhere, and it has been going on ever since the first flocking of the swallows back in July. Up to that time the season still seemed young; no one thought of harvest, of winter;—when there upon the telegraph wires one day were the swallows, and work against the winter had commenced.

The great migratory movements of the birds, mysterious in some of their courses as the currents of the sea, were in the beginning, and are still, for the most part, mere shifts to escape the cold. Why in the spring these same birds should leave the southern lands of plenty and travel back to the hungrier north to nest, is not easily explained. Perhaps it is the home instinct that draws them back; for home to birds (and men) is the land of the nest. However, it is very certain that among the autumn migrants there would be at once a great falling off should there come a series of warm open winters with abundance of food.

Bad as the weather is, there are a few of the seed-eating birds, like the quail, and some of the insect-eaters, like the chickadee, who are so well provided for that they can stay and survive the winter. But the great majority of the birds, because they have no storehouse nor barn, must take wing and fly away from the lean and hungry cold.

And I am glad to see them go. The thrilling honk of the flying wild geese out of the November sky tells me that the hollow forests and closing bays of the vast desolate north are empty now, except for the few creatures that find food and shelter in the snow. The wild geese pass, and I hear behind them the clang of the arctic gates, the boom of the bolt—then the long frozen silence. Yet it is not for long. Soon the bar will slip back, the gates will swing wide, and the wild geese will come honking over, swift to the greening marshes of the arctic bays once more.

Here in my own small woods and marshes there is much getting ready, much comforting assurance that Nature is quite equal to herself, that winter is not approaching unawares. There will be great lack, no doubt, before there is plenty again; there will be suffering and death. But what with the migrating, the strange deep sleeping, the building and harvesting, there will be also much comfortable, much joyous and sociable living.

Long before the muskrats began to build, even before the swallows commenced to flock, my chipmunks started their winter stores. I don't know which began his work first, which kept harder at it, chipmunk or the provident ant. The ant has come by a reputation for thrift, which, though entirely deserved, is still not the exceptional virtue it is made to seem. Chipmunk is just as thrifty. So is the busy bee. It is the thought of approaching winter that keeps the bee busy far beyond her summer needs. Much of her labor is entirely for the winter. By the first of August she has filled the brood chamber with honey—forty pounds of it, enough for the hatching bees and for the whole colony until the willows tassel again. But who knows what the winter may be? How cold and long drawn out into the coming May? So the harvesting is pushed with vigor on to the flowering of the last autumn asters—on until fifty, a hundred, or even three hundred pounds of surplus honey are sealed in the combs, and the colony is safe should the sun not shine again for a year and a day.

But here is Nature, in these extra pounds of honey, making preparation for me, incapable drone that I am. I could not make a drop of honey from a whole forest of linden bloom. Yet I must live, so I give the bees a bigger gum log than they need; I build them greater barns; and when the harvest is all in, this extra store I make my own. I too with the others am getting ready for the cold.

It is well that I am. The last of the asters have long since gone; so have the witch-hazels. All is quiet about the hives. The bees have formed into their warm winter clusters upon the combs, and except "when come the calm, mild days," they will fly no more until March or April. I will contract their entrances,—put on their storm-doors. And now there is little else that I can do but put on my own.

The whole of my out-of-doors is a great hive, stored and sealed for the winter, its swarming life close-clustered, and covering in its centre, as coals in the ashes, the warm life-fires of summer.

I stand along the edge of the hillside here and look down the length of its frozen slope. The brown leaves have drifted into the entrances, as if every burrow were forsaken; sand and sticks have washed in, too, littering and choking the doorways.

There is no sign of life. A stranger would find it hard to believe that my whole drove of forty-six ground hogs (wood-chucks) are gently snoring at the bottoms of these old un-interesting holes. Yet here they are, and quite out of danger, sleeping the sleep of the furry, the fat, and the forgetful.

The woodchuck's is a curious shift, a case of Nature outdoing herself. Winter spreads far and fast, and Woodchuck, in order to keep ahead out of danger, would need wings. But he wasn't given any. Must he perish then? Winter spreads far, but does not go deep—down only about four feet; and Woodchuck, if he cannot escape overland, can, perhaps, *under*land. So down he goes *through* the winter, down into a mild and even temperature, five long feet away—but as far away from the snow and cold as Bobolink among the reeds of the distant Orinoco.

Indeed, Woodchuck's is a farther journey and even more wonderful than Bobolink's, for these five feet carry him beyond the bounds of time and space into the mysterious realm of sleep, of suspended life, to the very gates of death. That he will return with Bobolink, that he will come up alive with the spring out of this dark way, is very strange.

For he went in most meagrely prepared. He took nothing with him, apparently. The muskrat built him a house, and under the spreading ice turned all the meadow into a well-stocked cellar. The beaver built a dam, cut and anchored under water a plenty of green sticks near his lodge, so that he too would be under cover when the ice formed, and have an abundance of tender bark at hand. Chipmunk spent half of his summer laying up food near his underground nest. But Woodchuck simply digged him a hole, a grave, then ate until no particle more of fat could be got into his baggy hide, and then crawled into his tomb, gave up the ghost, and waited the resurrection of the spring.

This is his shift! This is the length to which he goes, because he has no wings, and because he cannot cut, cure, and mow away in the depths of the stony hillside, enough clover hay to last him over the winter. The beaver cans his fresh food in cold water; the chipmunk selects long-keeping things and buries them; the woodchuck makes of himself a silo, eats all his winter hay in the summer while it is green, turns it at once into a surplus of himself, then buries that self, feeds upon it, and sleeps—and lives!

> The north wind doth blow,
> And we shall have snow,

but what good reason is there for our being daunted at the prospect? Robin and all the others are well prepared. Even the wingless frog, who is also lacking in fur and feathers and fat, even he has no care at the sound of the cold winds. Nature provides for him too, in her way, which is neither the way for the robin, the muskrat, nor the woodchuck. He survives, and all he has to do about it is to dig into the mud at the bottom of the ditch. This looks at first like the journey Woodchuck takes. But it is really a longer, stranger journey than Woodchuck's, for it takes the frog far beyond the realms of mere sleep, on into the cold, black land where no one can tell the quick from the dead.

The frost may or may not reach him here in the ooze. No matter. If the cold works down and freezes him into the mud, he never knows. But he will thaw out as good as new; he will sing again for joy and love as soon as his heart warms up enough to beat.

I have seen frogs frozen into the middle of solid lumps of ice in the laboratory. Drop the lump on the floor, and the frog would break out like a fragment of the ice itself. And this has happened more than once to the same frog without causing him the least apparent suffering or inconvenience. He would come to, and croak, and look as wise as ever.

> The north wind *may* blow,

but the muskrats are building; and it is by no means a cheerless prospect, this wood-and-meadow world of mine in the gray November light. The frost will not fall to-night as falls the plague on men; the brightness of the summer is gone, yet this chill gloom is not the sombre shadow of a pall. Nothing is dying in the fields: the grass-blades are wilting, the old leaves are falling, but no square foot of greensward will the winter kill, nor a single tree perhaps in my woodlot. There will be no less of life next April because of this winter, unless, perchance, conditions altogether exceptional starve some of the winter birds. These suffer most; yet as the seasons go, life even for the winter birds is comfortable and abundant.

The fence-rows and old pastures are full of berries that will keep the fires burning in the quail and partridge during the bitterest weather. Last February, however, I came upon two partridges in the snow, dead of hunger and cold. It was after an extremely long severe spell. But this was not all. These two birds since fall had been feeding regularly in the dried fodder corn that stood shocked over the field. One day all the corn was carted away. The birds found their supply of food suddenly cut off, and, unused to foraging the fence-rows and tangles for wild seeds, they seem to have given up the struggle at once, although within easy reach of plenty.

Hardly a minute's flight away was a great thicket of dwarf sumac covered with berries; there were bayberries, rose hips, green brier, bittersweet, black alder, and checkerberries—hillsides of the latter—that they might have found. These were hard fare, doubtless, after an unstinted supply of sweet corn; but still they were plentiful, and would have been sufficient had the birds made use of them.

The smaller birds of the winter, like the tree sparrow and junco, feed upon the weeds and grasses that ripen unmolested along the roadsides and waste places. A mixed flock of these small birds lived several days last winter upon the seeds of the ragweed in my mowing. The weeds came up in the early fall after the field was laid down to clover and timothy. They threatened to choke out the grass. I looked at them, rising shoulder-high and seedy over the greening field, and thought with dismay of how they would cover it by the next fall. After a time the snow came, a foot and a half of it, till only the tops of the seedy ragweeds showed above the level white; then the juncos, goldfinches, and tree sparrows came, and there was a five-day shucking of ragweed-seed in the mowing, and five days of life and plenty.

Then I looked and thought again—that, perhaps, into the original divine scheme of things were put even ragweeds. But then, perhaps, there was no original divine scheme of things. I don't know. As I watch the changing seasons, however, across the changeless years, I seem to find a scheme, a plan, a purpose, and there are weeds and winters in it, and it seems divine.

The muskrats are building; the last of the migrating geese have gone over; the wild mice have harvested their acorns; the bees have clustered; the woodchucks are asleep; and the sap in the big hickory by the side of the house has crept down out of reach of the fingers of the frost. I will put on the storm-doors and the double windows. Even now the logs are blazing cheerily on the wide, warm hearth.

II

Christmas in the Woods

ON the night before this particular Christmas every creature of the woods that could stir was up and stirring, for over
the old snow was falling swiftly, silently, a soft, fresh covering
that might mean a hungry Christmas unless the dinner were
had before morning.

But when the morning dawned, a cheery Christmas sun
broke across the great gum swamp, lighting the snowy boles
and soft-piled limbs of the giant trees with indescribable glory,
and pouring, a golden flood, into the deep spongy bottoms
below. It would be a perfect Christmas in the woods, clear,
mild, stirless, with silent footing for me, and everywhere the
telltale snow.

And everywhere the Christmas spirit, too. As I paused among the pointed cedars of the pasture, looking down into the cripple at the head of the swamp, a clear wild whistle rang in the thicket, followed by a flash through the alders like a tongue of fire, as a cardinal grosbeak shot down to the tangle of greenbrier and magnolia under the slope. It was a fleck of flaming summer. As warm as summer, too, the stag-horn sumac burned on the crest of the ridge against the group of holly trees,—trees as fresh as April, and all aglow with berries. The woods were decorated for the holy day. The gentleness of the soft new snow touched everything; cheer and good-will lighted the unclouded sky and warmed the thick depths of the evergreens, and blazed in the crimson-berried bushes of the ilex and alder. The Christmas woods were glad.

Nor was the gladness all show, mere decoration. There was real cheer in abundance, for I was back in the old home woods, back along the Cohansey, back where you can pick persimmons off the trees at Christmas. There are persons who say the Lord might have made a better berry than the strawberry, but He didn't. Perhaps He didn't make the strawberry at all. But He did make the Cohansey Creek persimmon, and He made it as good as He could. Nowhere else under the sun can you find such persimmons as these along the creek, such richness of flavor, such gummy, candied quality, woodsy, wild, crude,—especially the fruit of two particular trees on the west bank, near Lupton's Pond. But they never come to this perfection, never quite lose their pucker, until midwinter,—as if they had been intended for the Christmas table of the woods.

It had been nearly twenty years since I crossed this pasture of the cedars on my way to the persimmon trees. The cows had been crossing every year, yet not a single new crook had they worn in the old paths. But I was half afraid as I came to the fence where I could look down upon the pond and over to the persimmon trees. Not one of the Luptons, who owned pasture and pond and trees, had ever been a boy, so far as I could remember, or had ever eaten of those persimmons. Would they have left the trees through all these years?

I pushed through the hedge of cedars and stopped for an instant, confused. The very pond was gone! and the trees! No, there was the pond,—but how small the patch of water! and the two persimmon trees? The bush and undergrowth had grown these twenty years. Which way? Ah, there they stand, only their leafless tops showing; but see the hard angular limbs, how closely globed with fruit! how softly etched upon the sky!

I hurried around to the trees and climbed the one with the two broken branches, up, clear up to the top, into the thick of the persimmons.

Did I say it had been twenty years? That could not be. Twenty years would have made me a man, and this sweet, real taste in my mouth only a *boy* could know. But there was college, and marriage, a Massachusetts farm, four boys of my own, and—no matter! it could not have been *years*—twenty years—since. It was only yesterday that I last climbed this tree and ate the rich rimy fruit frosted with a Christmas snow.

And yet, could it have been yesterday? It was storming, and I clung here in the swirling snow and heard the wild ducks go over in their hurry toward the bay. Yesterday, and all this change in the vast treetop world, this huddled pond, those narrowed meadows, that shrunken creek! I should have eaten the persimmons and climbed straight down, not stopped to gaze out upon the pond, and away over the dark ditches to the creek.

But reaching out quickly I gathered another handful,—and all was yesterday again.

I filled both pockets of my coat and climbed down. I kept those persimmons and am tasting them to-night. Lupton's Pond may fill to a puddle, the meadows may shrivel, the creek dry up and disappear, and old Time may even try his wiles on me. But I shall foil him to the end; for I am carrying still in my pocket some of yesterday's persimmons,—persimmons that ripened in the rime of a winter when I was a boy.

High and alone in a bare persimmon tree for one's dinner hardly sounds like a merry Christmas. But I was not alone. I had noted the fresh tracks beneath the tree before I climbed up, and now I saw that the snow had been partly brushed from several of the large limbs as the 'possum had moved about in the tree for his Christmas dinner. We were guests at the same festive board, and both of us at Nature's invitation. It mattered not that the 'possum had eaten and gone this hour or more. Such is good form in the woods. He was expecting me, so he came early, out of modesty, and, that I too might be entirely at my ease, he departed early, leaving his greetings for me in the snow.

Thus I was not alone; here was good company and plenty of it. I never lack a companion in the woods when I can pick up a trail. The 'possum and I ate together. And this was just the fellowship I needed, this sharing the persimmons with the 'possum. I had broken bread, not with the 'possum only, but with all the out-of-doors. I was now fit to enter the woods, for I was filled with good-will and persimmons, as full as the 'possum; and putting myself under his gentle guidance, I got down upon the ground, took up his clumsy trail, and descended toward the swamp. Such an entry is one of the particular joys of the winter. To go in with a fox, a mink, or a 'possum through the door of the woods is to find yourself at home. Any one can get inside the out-of-doors, as the grocery boy or the census man gets inside our houses. You can bolt in at any time on business. A trail, however, is Nature's invitation. There may be other, better beaten paths for mere feet. But go softly with the 'possum, and at the threshold you are met by the spirit of the wood, you are made the guest of the open, silent, secret out-of-doors.

I went down with the 'possum. He had traveled home leisurely and without fear, as his tracks plainly showed. He was full of persimmons. A good happy world this, where such fare could be had for the picking! What need to hurry home, except one were in danger of falling asleep by the way? So I thought, too, as I followed his winding path; and if I was tracking him to his den, it was only to wake him for a moment with the compliments of the season. But it was not even a momentary disturbance; for when I finally found him in his hollow gum, he was sound asleep, and only half realized that some one was poking him gently in the ribs and wishing him a merry Christmas.

The 'possum had led me to the centre of the empty, hollow swamp, where the great-boled gums lifted their branches like a timbered, unshingled roof between me and the wide sky. Far away through the spaces of the rafters I saw a pair of wheeling buzzards, and under them, in lesser circles, a broad-winged hawk. Here, at the feet of the tall, clean trees, looking up through the leafless limbs, I had something of a measure for the flight of the birds. The majesty and the mystery of the distant buoyant wings were singularly impressive.

I have seen the turkey-buzzard sailing the skies on the bitterest winter days. To-day, however, could hardly be called winter.

Indeed, nothing yet had felt the pinch of the cold. There was no hunger yet in the swamp, though this new snow had scared the raccoons out, and their half-human tracks along the margin of the swamp stream showed that, if not hungry, they at least feared that they might be.

For a coon hates snow. He will invariably sleep off the first light snowfalls, and even in the late winter he will not venture forth in fresh snow unless driven by hunger or some other dire need. Perhaps, like a cat or a hen, he dislikes the wetting of his feet. Or it may be that the soft snow makes bad hunting—for him. The truth is, I believe, that such a snow makes too good hunting for the dogs and the gunner. The new snow tells too clear a story. His home is no inaccessible den among the ledges; only a hollow in some ancient oak or tupelo. Once within, he is safe from the dogs, but the long fierce fight for life taught him generations ago that the nest-tree is a fatal trap when behind the dogs come the axe and the gun. So he has grown wary and enduring. He waits until the snow grows crusty, when without sign, and almost without scent, he can slip forth among the long shadows and prowl to the edge of dawn.

Skirting the stream out toward the higher back woods, I chanced to spy a bunch of snow in one of the great sour gums that I thought was an old nest. A second look showed me tiny green leaves, then white berries, then mistletoe.

It was not a surprise, for I had found it here before,—a long, long time before. It was back in my schoolboy days, back beyond those twenty years, that I first stood here under the mistletoe and had my first romance. There was no chandelier, no pretty girl, in that romance,—only a boy, the mistletoe, the giant trees, and the sombre silent swamp. Then there was his discovery, the thrill of deep delight, and the wonder of his knowledge of the strange unnatural plant! All plants had been plants to him until, one day, he read the life of the mistletoe. But that was English mistletoe; so the boy's wonder world of plant life was still as far away as Mars, when, rambling alone through the swamp along the creek, he stopped under a big curious bunch of green, high up in one of the gums, and— made his first discovery.

So the boy climbed up again this Christmas Day at the peril of his precious neck, and brought down a bit of that old romance.

I followed the stream along through the swamp to the open meadows, and then on under the steep wooded hillside that ran up to the higher land of corn and melon fields. Here at the foot of the slope the winter sun lay warm, and here in the sheltered briery border I came upon the Christmas birds.

There was a great variety of them, feeding and preening and chirping in the vines. The tangle was a-twitter with their quiet, cheery talk. Such a medley of notes you could not hear at any other season outside a city bird store. How far the different species understood one another I should like to know, and whether the hum of voices meant sociability to them, as it certainly meant to me. Doubtless the first cause of their flocking here was the sheltered warmth and the great numbers of berry-laden bushes, for there was no lack either of abundance or variety on the Christmas table.

In sight from where I stood hung bunches of withering chicken or frost grapes, plump clusters of blue-black berries of the greenbrier, and limbs of the smooth winterberry bending with their flaming fruit. There were bushes of crimson ilex, too, trees of fruiting dogwood and holly, cedars in berry, dwarf sumac and seedy sedges, while patches on the wood slopes uncovered by the sun were spread with trailing partridge berry and the coral-fruited wintergreen. I had eaten part of my dinner with the 'possum; I picked a quantity of these wintergreen berries, and continued my meal with the birds. And they also had enough and to spare.

Among the birds in the tangle was a large flock of northern fox sparrows, whose vigorous and continuous scratching in the bared spots made a most lively and cheery commotion. Many of them were splashing about in tiny pools of snow-water, melted partly by the sun and partly by the warmth of their bodies as they bathed. One would hop to a softening bit of snow at the base of a tussock, keel over and begin to flop, soon sending up a shower of sparkling drops from his rather chilly tub. A winter snow-water bath seemed a necessity, a luxury indeed, for they all indulged, splashing with the same purpose and zest that they put into their scratching among the leaves.

A much bigger splashing drew me quietly through the bushes to find a marsh hawk giving himself a Christmas souse. The scratching, washing, and talking of the birds; the masses of green in the cedars, holly, and laurels; the glowing colors of the berries against the snow; the blue of the sky, and the golden warmth of the light made Christmas in the heart of the noon that the very swamp seemed to feel.

Three months later there was to be scant picking here, for this was the beginning of the severest winter I ever knew. From this very ridge, in February, I had reports of berries gone, of birds starving, of whole coveys of quail frozen dead in the snow; but neither the birds nor I dreamed to-day of any such hunger and death. A flock of robins whirled into the cedars above me; a pair of cardinals whistled back and forth; tree sparrows, juncos, nuthatches, chickadees, and cedar-birds cheeped among the trees and bushes; and from the farm lands at the top of the slope rang the calls of meadowlarks.

Halfway up the hill I stopped under a blackjack oak, where, in the thin snow, there were signs of something like a Christmas revel. The ground was sprinkled with acorn shells and trampled over with feet of several kinds and sizes,—quail, jay, and partridge feet; rabbit, squirrel, and mice feet, all over the snow as the feast of acorns had gone on. Hundreds of the acorns were lying about, gnawed away at the cup end, where the shell was thinnest, many of them further broken and cleaned out by the birds.

As I sat studying the signs in the snow, my eye caught a tiny trail leading out from the others straight away toward a broken pile of cord-wood. The tracks were planted one after the other, so directly in line as to seem like the prints of a single foot. "That's a weasel's trail," I said, "the death's-head at this feast," and followed it slowly to the wood. A shiver crept over me as I felt, even sooner than I saw, a pair of small sinister eyes fixed upon mine. The evil pointed head, heavy but alert, and with a suggestion of fierce strength out of all relation to the slender body, was watching me from between the sticks of cord-wood. And so he had been watching the mice and birds and rabbits feasting under the tree!

I packed a ball of snow round and hard, slipped forward upon my knees, and hurled it. "Spat!" it struck the end of a stick within an inch of the ugly head, filling the crevice with snow. Instantly the head appeared at another crack, and another ball struck viciously beside it. Now it was back where it first appeared, and did not flinch for the next, nor the next ball. The third went true, striking with a "chug" and packing the crack. But the black, hating eyes were still watching me a foot lower down.

It is not all peace and good-will in the Christmas woods. But there is more of peace and good-will than of any other spirit. The weasels are few. More friendly and timid eyes were watching me than bold and murderous. It was foolish to want to kill—even the weasel. For one's woods are what one makes them, and so I let the man with the gun, who chanced along, think that I had turned boy again, and was snowballing the woodpile, just for the fun of trying to hit the end of the biggest stick.

I was glad he had come. As he strode off with his stained bag I felt kindlier toward the weasel. There were worse in the woods than he,—worse, because all of their killing was pastime. The weasel must kill to live, and if he gloated over the kill, why, what fault of his? But the other weasel, the one with the blood-stained bag, he killed for the love of killing. I was glad he was gone.

The crows were winging over toward their great roost in the pines when I turned toward the town. They, too, had had good picking along the creek flats and ditches of the meadows. Their powerful wing-beats and constant play told of full crops and no fear for the night, already softly gray across the white silent fields. The air was crisper; the snow began to crackle under foot; the twigs creaked and rattled as I brushed along; a brown beech leaf wavered down and skated with a thin scratch over crust; and pure as the snow-wrapped crystal world, and sweet as the soft gray twilight, came the call of a quail.

The voices, colors, odors, and forms of summer were gone. The very face of things had changed; all had been reduced, made plain, simple, single, pure! There was less for the senses, but how much keener now their joy! The wide landscape, the frosty air, the tinkle of tiny icicles, and, out of the quiet of the falling twilight, the voice of the quail!

There is no day but is beautiful in the woods; and none more beautiful than one like this Christmas Day,—warm and still and wrapped, to the round red berries of the holly, in the magic of the snow.

III
𝔄 Cure for 𝔚inter

For, lo, the winter is past,
The rain is over and gone—

yet the snow lies white upon the fields, my little river huddles
under the ice, and a new calendar hangs against the faded wall.
But the storm is spent, the sun is out, there is a cheery *drip,
drip, drip* from the eaves, eggs are sixty cents a dozen, and I
am writing to the golden cackle of my hens. New Year's Day,
and winter gone! No, not quite gone, with eggs at such a price;
still, it must be plain to every one that I can have but little of
winter left: eggs are liable to come down any day.

It would be different, of course, were I buying eggs at sixty
cents,—all the difference between a winter-sick and a winter-
well condition. Selling eggs for sixty cents is a cure, though
not for poverty when one has only thirty hens; but it is a cure
for winter. The virtue, however, is not in the sixty cents. There
is no cure for winter in mere money. The virtue is in the eggs,
or, perhaps, it is really found in keeping the hens.

Keeping the hens, and the two pigs, the horse, the cow, the four boys, and the farm, for the year around, is a sure cure for winter, and for a great many other ills. In addition to the farm, one must have some kind of a salary, and a real love for nature; but given the boys and the farm, the love will come, for it lies dormant in human nature, as certain seeds seem to lie dormant in the soil; and as for the salary, one must have a salary—farm or flat.

The prescription, then, should read:—

℞

A small farm—of an acre or more,
A small income—of a thousand or more,
A small family—of four boys or more,
A real love of nature.

Sig. Morning and evening chores. The dose to be taken daily, as long as winter lasts.

This will cure. It is an old-fashioned household mixture that can be compounded in any country kitchen. But that is the trouble with it,—it is a *home* remedy that cannot be bought of the apothecary. There is more trouble with it, too, largely on account of the regularity with which milking time returns and the dose of chores. But it is effective. A farm and congenial chores are a sovereign cure for uncongenial time.

Here on the farm the signs of coming winter are not ominous signs. The pensive, mellowing days of early autumn have been preparing the garden and your mind for the shock of the first frost. Once past this and winter is welcome; it becomes a physical, spiritual need. The blood reddens at the promise of it; the soul turns comfortingly in and finds itself; and the digging of the potatoes commences, and the shocking of the corn, the picking of the apples, the piling up on the sunny side of the barn of the big golden squashes.

A single golden squash holds over almost enough of the summer to keep a long winter away from the farm; and the six of them in the attic, filling the rafter room with sunshine, never allow the hoary old monarch to show more than his face at the skylight. Pie is not the only thing one brings in with his winter squashes. He stores the ripe September in their wrinkled rinds, rinds that are ridged and bossy with the summer's gold.

To dig one's own potatoes! to shock one's own corn! to pick one's own apples! to pile one's own squashes at one's own barn! It is like filling one's system with an antitoxin before going into a fever-plagued country. One is immune to winter after this, provided he stays to bake his apples in his own wood fire. One works himself into a glow with all this digging, and picking, and piling that lasts until warm weather comes again; and along with this harvest glow comes stealing over him the after-harvest peace. It is the serenity of Indian summer, the mood of the after-harvest season, upon him,—upon him and his fields and woods.

The stores are all in: the acorns have ripened and lie hidden where the squirrels will forget some of them, but where none of the forgotten will forget to grow; the winged seeds of the asters have drifted down the highways, over the hillsides and meadows; the birds are gone; the muskrats' lodge is all but finished; the hickories and the leaf-hid hepaticas are budded against the coming spring. All is ready, all is safe,—the stores are all in. Quiet and a golden peace lie warm upon the fields. It is Indian summer.

Such a mood is a necessary condition for the cure. Such a

mood *is* the cure, indeed, for such a mood means harmony with earth and sky, and every wind that blows. In all his physical life man is as much a part of Nature, and as subject to her inexorable laws, as the fields and the trees and the birds. I have seen a maple growing out of the pavement of a city street, but no such maple as stands yonder at the centre of my neighbor's meadow. I lived and grew on the same street with the maple; but not as I live and grow here on the farm. Only on a farm does a man live in a normal, natural environment, only here can he comply with all the demands of Nature, can he find a cure for winter.

To Nature man is just as precious as a woodchuck or a sparrow, but not more. She cares for the woodchuck as long as he behaves like a woodchuck; so she cares for the sparrow, the oyster, the orchid, and for man. But he must behave like a natural man, must live where she intended him to live, and at the approach of winter he must neither hibernate nor migrate, for he is what the naturalists call a "winter resident." It is not in his nature to fly away nor to go to sleep, but, like the red squirrel and the muskrat, to prepare to live up all the winter. So his original, unperverted animal instinct leads him to store.

Long ago he buried his provisions in pits and hung them up on poles. Even his vocabulary he gathered together as his word-hoard. He is still possessed of the remnant of the instinct; he will still store. Cage him in a city, give him more than he needs for winter, relieve him of all possibility of want, and yet he will store. You cannot cage an instinct nor eradicate it. It will be obeyed, if all that can be found in the way of pit and pole be a grated vault in the deep recesses of some city bank.

Cage a red squirrel and he will store in the cage; so will the white-footed mouse. Give the mouse more than he can

use, put him in a cellar, where there is enough already stored
for a city of mice, and he will take from your piles and make
piles of his own. He must store or be unhappy and undone.

A white-footed mouse got into my cellar last winter and
found it, like the cellar of the country mouse in the fable,—

> Full benely stuffit, baith but and ben,
> Of beirris and nuttis, peis, ry and quheit—

all of it, ready stored, so that,

> Quhen ever scho list scho had aneuch to eit.

Enough to eat? Certainly; but is enough to eat all that a mouse
wants? So far from being satisfied with mere meat was this
particular mouse, that finding herself in the cellar in the midst
of plenty, she at once began to carry my winter stores from
where I had put them, and to make little heaps for herself in
every dark cranny and corner of the cellar. A pint, or less, of
"nuttis"—shagbarks—she tucked away in the toe of my hunting
boot. The nuts had been left in a basket in the vegetable cellar;
the boots stood out by the chimney in the furnace room, and
there were double doors and a brick partition wall between.
No matter. Here were the nuts she had not yet stored, and
out yonder was the hole, smooth and deep and dark, to store
them in. She found a way past the partition wall.

Every morning I shook those nuts out of my boot and
sent them rattling over the cellar floor. Every night the mouse
gathered them up and put them snugly back into the toe of
the boot. She could not have carried more than one nut at a
time,—up the tall boot-leg and down the oily, slippery inside.

I should have liked to see her scurrying about the cellar, looking after her curiously difficult harvest. Apparently, they were new nuts to her every evening. Once or twice I came down to find them lying untouched. The mouse, perhaps, was away over night on other business. But the following night they were all gathered and nicely packed in the boot as before. And as before I sent them sixty ways among the barrels and boxes of the furnace room. But I did it once too often, for it dawned upon the mouse one night that these were the same old nuts that she had gathered now a dozen times; and that night they disappeared. Where? I wondered. Weeks passed, and I had entirely forgotten about the nuts, when I came upon them, the identical nuts of my boot, tiered carefully up in a corner of the deep, empty water-tank away off in the attic.

Store? The mouse had to store. She had to, not to feed her body,—there was plenty in the cellar for that,—but to satisfy her soul. A mouse's soul, that something within a mouse which makes for more than meat, may not be a soul at all, but only a bundle of blind instincts. The human soul, that thing whose satisfaction is so often a box of chocolates and a silk petticoat, may be better and higher than the soul of a mouse, may be a different thing indeed; but originally it, too, had simple, healthful instincts; and among them, atrophied now, but not wholly gone, may still be found the desire for a life that is more than something to eat and something to put on.

To be sure, here on the farm, one may eat all of his potatoes, his corn, his beans and squashes before the long, lean winter comes to an end. But if squashes *to eat* were all, then he could buy squashes, bigger, fairer, fatter ones, and at less cost, no doubt, at the grocery store. He may need to eat the squash, but what he needs more, and cannot buy, is the raising of it, the harvesting of it, the fathering of it. He needs to watch it grow, to pick it, to heft it, and have his neighbor heft it; to go up occasionally to the attic and look at it. He almost hates to *eat* it.

A man may live in the city and buy a squash and eat it. That is all he can do with a boughten squash; for a squash that he cannot raise, he cannot store, nor take delight in outside of pie. And can a man live where his garden is a grocery? his storehouse a grocery? his bins, cribs, mows, and attics so many pasteboard boxes, bottles, and tin cans? Tinned squash in pie may taste like any squash pie; but it is no longer squash; and is a squash nothing if not pie? Oh, but he gets a lithograph squash upon the can to show him how the pulp looked as God made it. This is a sop to his higher sensibilities; it is a commercial reminder, too, that life even in the city should be more than pie,—it is also the commercial way of preserving the flavor of the canned squash, else he would not know whether he were eating squash or pumpkin or sweet potato. But then it makes little difference, all things taste the same in the city,—all taste of tin.

There is a need in the nature of man for many things,—for a wife, a home, children, friends, and a need for winter. The wild goose feels it, too, and no length of domesticating can tame the wild desire to fly when the frosts begin to fall; the woodchuck feels it; carry him to the tropics and still he will sleep as though the snows of New England lay deep in the mouth of his burrow. The partridge's foot broadens at the approach of winter into a snowshoe; the ermine's fur turns snow-white. Winter is in their bones; it is good for them; it is health, not disease—with snowshoes provided and snow-colored fur.

Nature supplies her own remedies. Winter brings its own cure,—snowshoes and snowy coats, short days and long nights, the narrowed round, the widened view, the open fire, leisure, quiet, and the companionship of your books, your children, your wife, your own strange soul—here on the farm.

Where else does it come, bringing all of this? Where else are conditions such that all weather is good weather? The weather a man needs? Here he is planted like his trees; his roots are in the soil; the changing seasons are his life. He feeds upon them; works with them; rests in them; yields to them, and finds in their cycle more than the sum of his physical needs.

A man lives quite without roots in a city, like some of the orchids, hung up in the air; or oftener, like the mistletoe, rooted, but drawing his life parasitically from some simpler, stronger, fresher life planted far below him in the soil. There he cannot touch the earth and feed upon life's first sources. He knows little of any kind but bad weather. Summer is hot, winter is nasty, spring and autumn scarcely are at all, for they do not make him uncomfortable. The round year is four changes of clothes—and a tank-sprinkled, snow-choked, smoke-clouded, cobble-paved, wheel-wracked, street-scented, wire-lighted half-day, half-night something, that is neither spring, summer, autumn, nor winter.

A city is a sore on the face of Nature; not a dangerous, ugly sore, necessarily, if one can get out of it often enough and far enough, but a sore, nevertheless, that Nature will have nothing kindly to do with. The snows that roof my sheds with Carrara, that robe my trees with ermine, that spread close and warm over my mowing, that call out the sleds and the sleigh-bells, fall into the city streets as mud, as danger on the city roofs,—as a nuisance over the city's length and breadth,

a nuisance to be hauled off and dumped into the harbor as
fast as shovels and carts can move it.

But you cannot dump your winter and send it off to sea.
There is no cure for winter in a tip-cart; no cure in the city.
There is consolation in the city, for there is plenty of company
in the misery. But company really means more of the misery.
If life is to be endured, if all that one can do with winter is
to shovel it and suffer it, then to the city for the winter, for
there one's share of the shoveling is small, and the suffering
there seems very evenly distributed.

Here on the farm is neither shoveling nor suffering, no
quarrel whatever with the season. Here you have nothing to
do with its coming or going further than making preparation
to welcome it and to bid it farewell. You slide, instead, with
your boys; you do up the chores early in the short twilight,
pile the logs high by the blazing chimney and—you remember that there is to be a lecture to-night by the man who has
said it all in his book; there is to be a concert, a reception, a
club dinner, in the city, sixteen blissful miles away,—and it is
snowing! You can go if you have to. But the soft tapping on
the window-panes grows faster, the voices at the corners of
the house rise higher, shriller. You look down at your slippers,
poke up the fire, settle a little deeper into the big chair, and
beg Eve to go on with the reading.

And she reads on—

> Shut in from all the world without,
> We sat the clean-winged hearth about,
> Content to let the north wind roar
> In baffled rage at pane and door,
> While the red logs before us beat

The frost-line back with tropic heat;
And ever, when a louder blast
Shook beam and rafter as it passed,
The merrier up its roaring draught
The great throat of the chimney laughed.

* * * * * *

And, for the winter fireside meet,
Between the andirons' straddling feet,
The mug of cider simmered slow,
The apples sputtered in a row,
And, close at hand, the basket stood
With nuts from brown October's wood.

But you will be snow-bound in the morning and cannot get to town? Perhaps; but it happened so only twice to me in the long snowy winter of 1904. So twice we read the poem, and twice we lived the poem, and twice? yes, a thousand times, we were glad for a day at home that wasn't Sunday, for a whole long day to pop corn with the boys.

A farm, of all human habitations, is most of a home, and never so much of a home as in the winter when the stock and the crops are housed, when furrow and boundary fence are covered, when earth and sky conspire to drive a man indoors and to keep him in,—where he needs to stay for a while and be quiet.

No problem of city life is more serious than the problem of making in the city a home. A habitation where you can have no garden, no barn, no attic, no cellar, no chickens, no bees, no boys (we were allowed *one* boy by the janitor of our city flat), no fields, no sunset skies, no snow-bound days, can hardly be a home. To live in the fifth flat, at No. 6 West

Seventh Street, is not to have a home. Pictures on the walls, a fire in the grate, and a prayer in blending zephyrs over the door for God to bless the place can scarcely make of No. 6 more than a sum in arithmetic. There is no home environment about this fifth flat at No. 6, just as there is none about cell No. 6, in the fifth tier of the west corridor of the Tombs.

The idea, the concept, home, is a house set back from the road behind a hedge of trees, a house with a yard, with flowers, chickens, and a garden,—a country home. The songs of home are all of country homes:—

> How dear to this heart are the scenes of my childhood
> When fond recollection presents them to view:
>   * * * * * *
> The gutter, the lamp-post, the curb that ran by it,
> And e'en the brass spigot that did for a well.—

Impossible! You cannot sing of No. 6, West Seventh, fifth flight up. And what of a home that cannot be remembered as a song! It is not a home, but only a floor over your head, a floor under your feet, a hole in the wall of the street, a burrow into which you are dumped by a hoisting machine. It is warm inside; Eve is with you, and the baby, and your books. But you do not hear the patter of the rain upon the roof, nor the murmur of the wind in the trees; you do not see the sun go down beyond the wooded hills, nor ever feel the quiet of the stars. You have no largeness round about you; you are the centre of nothing; you have no garden, no harvest, no chores,—no home! There is not room enough about a city flat for a home, nor chores enough in city life for a living.

For a man's life consisteth not in an abundance of things,

but in the particular kind and number of his chores. A chore is a fragment of real life that is lived with the doing. All real living must be lived; it cannot be bought or hired. And herein is another serious problem in city life,—it is the tragedy of city life that it is so nearly all lived for us. We hire Tom, Dick, and Harry to live it; we buy it of the butcher, the baker, the candlestick-maker. It is not so here on the farm; for here one has the full round of life's chores, and here, on a professor's salary, one may do all the chores himself.

We may hire our praying and our thinking done for us and still live; but not our chores. They are to the life of the spirit what breathing and eating and sleeping are to the life of the body. Not to feed your own horse is to miss the finest joy of having a horse,—the friendship of the noble creature; not to "pick up" the eggs yourself, nor hoe your own garden, nor play with your own boys! Why, what is the use of having boys if you are never going to be "it" again, if you are not to be a boy once more along with them!

There are some things, the making of our clothes, perhaps, that we must hire done for us. But clothes are not primitive and essential; they are accidental, an adjunct, a necessary adjunct, it may be, but belonging to a different category from children, gardens, domestic animals, and a domestic home. And yet, how much less cloth we should need, and what a saving, too, of life's selvage, could we return to the spinning-wheel and loom as we go back to the farm and the daily chores!

> She, harvest done, to char work did aspire,
> Meat, drink, and twopence were her daily hire.

And who has not known the same aspiration? has not had a

longing for mere chores, and their ample compensation? It is such a reasonable, restful, satisfying aspiration! Harvest done! Done the work and worry of the day! Then the twilight, and the evening chores, and the soft closing of the door! At dawn we shall go forth again until the evening; but with a better spirit for our labor after the fine discipline of the morning chores. The day should start and stop in our own selves; labor should begin and come to an end in the responsibility of the wholesome, homely round of our own chores.

Summer is gone, the harvest is done, and winter is passing on its swiftest days. So swift, indeed, are the days that morning and evening meet, bound up like a sheaf by the circle of the chores. For there is never an end to the chores; never a time when they are all done; never a day when the round of them is not to be done again. And herein lies more of their virtue as a winter cure.

Life is not busier here than elsewhere; time is not swifter, but more enjoyable, because so much of life is left unfinished and time is thrown so much more into the future. There is no past on the farm; it is all to come; no sure defeat, but always promise; no settled winter, but always the signs of coming spring.

To-day is the first of January, snowy, brilliant, but dripping with the sound of spring wherever the sun lies warm, and calling with the heart of spring yonder where the crows are flocking. There is spring in the talk of the chickadees outside my window, and in the cheerful bluster of a red squirrel in the hickory. No bluebird has returned yet: spring is not here, not quite, I hope, but it is coming, and so near that I shall drop my pen and go out to the barn to put together some new beehives, for I must have them ready for the spring. Winter!

The winter is almost gone. Why, it is barely a month since I brought my bees into the cellar, and here I am taking them out again—in prospect.

The hives have just come from the factory "in the flat": sawed, planed, dovetailed, and matched,—a delightful set of big blocks,—ready to be nailed together. You feel a bit mean, keeping them from the children. But the oldest of the boys is only six, and he had a walking bear for Christmas. Besides, when you were a *little* boy you never had many blocks, and never a walking bear. So you keep the hives. And how suddenly the January day goes! You hammer on into the deepening dusk, and the chickens go to roost without their supper. You would have hammered on all night, but the hives ran out. Five hives won't last very long; and you sigh as they stand finished. You could wish them all in pieces to do over again, so smooth the stock, so fragrant the piny smell, so accurate and nice the parts from cover to bottom board!

Winter! with January started, and February two days short! It is all a fiction. You had dreams of long evenings, of books and crackling fires, and of days shut in. It still snows; there is something still left of the nights, but not half enough, for the seed catalogues are already beginning to arrive.

The snow lies a foot deep over the strawberry bed and the frozen soil where the potatoes are to be. Yet the garden grows—on paper? No, not on paper, but in your own eager soul. The joy of a garden is as real in January as in June.

And so the winter goes. For if it is not the garden and the bees, it is some of a thousand other chores that keep you busy and living past the present,—and past the present is the spring.

I am watching for the phœbes to return to the shed,—they are my first birds. I long to hear the shrill piping of the March frogs, to pick a blue hepatica from beneath the pines; for these are some of the things, besides cheaper rent, more room, more boys, fresh air, quiet, and a cow, that one lives for here on the farm. But I am not waiting, winter-sick, for I have stored the summer in attic and cellar; I am already having my spring—in prospect; and as for the actual winter, the snow-bound days are all too few for the real winter joys of this simple, ample life, here in the quiet, among the neighbor fields.

IV

The Nature-Student

I

I HAD made a nice piece of dissection, a pretty demonstration—for a junior.

"You didn't know a dog was put together so beautifully, did you?" said the professor, frankly enjoying the sight of the marvelous system of nerves laid bare by the knife. "Now, see here," he went on, eyeing me keenly, "doesn't a revelation like that take all the moonshine about the 'beauties of nature' clean out of you?"

I looked at the lifeless lump upon my table, and answered very deliberately: "No, it doesn't. That's a fearful piece of mechanism. I appreciate that. But what is any system of nerves or muscles—mere dead dog—compared with the love and affection of the dog alive?"

The professor was trying to make a biologist out of me. He had worked faithfully, but I had persisted in a very unscientific love for live dog. Not that I didn't enjoy comparative anatomy, for I did. The problem of concrescence or differentiation in the cod's egg also was intensely interesting to me. And so was the sight and the suggestion of the herring as they crowded up the run on their way to the spawning pond. The professor had lost patience. I don't blame him.

"Well," he said, turning abruptly, "you had better quit. You'll be only a biological fifth wheel."

I quit. Here on my table lies the scalpel. Since that day it has only sharpened lead pencils.

Now a somewhat extensive acquaintance with scientific folk leads me to believe that the attitude of my professor toward the out-of-doors is not exceptional. The love for nature is all moonshine, all maudlin sentiment. Even those like my professor, who have to do with out-of-door life and conditions,—zoölogists, botanists, geologists,—look upon naturalists, and others who love birds and fields, as of a kind with those harmless but useless inanities who collect tobacco tags, postage stamps, and picture postal cards. Sentiment is not scientific.

I have a biological friend, a professor of zoölogy, who never saw a woodchuck in the flesh. He would not know a woodchuck with the fur on from a mongoose. Not until he had skinned it and set up the skeleton could he pronounce it *Arctomys monax* with certainty. Yes, he could tell by the teeth. Dentition is a great thing. He could tell a white pine (*strobus*) from a pitch pine (*rigida*) by just a cone and a bundle of needles,—one has five, the other three, to the bundle. But he wouldn't recognize a columned aisle of the one from a Jersey barren of the other. That is not the worst of it: he would not see even the aisle or the barren,—only trees.

As we jogged along recently, on a soft midwinter day that

followed a day of freezing, my little three-year-old threw his
nose into the air and cried: "Oh, fader, I smell de pitch pines,
de scraggly pines,—'ou calls 'em Joisey pines!" And sure
enough, around a double curve in the road we came upon a
single clump of the scraggly pitch pines. Our drive had taken
us through miles of the common white species.

Did you ever smell the pitch pines when they are thawing
out? It is quite as healthful, if not as scientific, to recognize
them by their resinous breath as by their needles per bundle.

I want this small boy some time to know the difference
between these needle bundles. But I want him to learn now,
and to remember always, that the hard days are sure to soften,
and that then there oozes from the scraggly pitch pines a balm,
a piny, penetrating, purifying balm,—a tonic to the lungs, a
healing to the soul.

All foolishness? sentiment? moonshine?—this love for woods
and fields, this need I have for companionship with birds and
trees, this longing for the feel of grass and the smell of earth?
When I told my biological friend that these longings were
real and vital, as vital as the highest problems of the stars and
the deepest questions of life, he pitied me, but made no reply.

He sees clearly a difference between live and dead men, a
difference between the pleasure he gets from the society of his
friends, and the knowledge, interesting as it may be, which
he obtains in a dissecting-room. But he sees no such difference between live and dead nature, nature in the fields and
in the laboratory. Nature is all a biological problem to him,
not a quick thing,—a shape, a million shapes, informed with
spirit,—a voice of gladness, a mild and healing sympathy, a
companionable soul.

"But there you go!" he exclaims, "talking poetry again. Why

don't you deal with facts? What do you mean by nature-study, love for the out-of-doors, anyway!"

I do not mean a sixteen weeks' course in zoölogy, or botany, or in Wordsworth. I mean, rather, a gentle life course in getting acquainted with the toads and stars that sing together, for most of us, just within and above our own dooryards. It is a long life course in the deep and beautiful things of living nature,—the nature we know so well as a corpse. It is of necessity a somewhat unsystematized, incidental, vacation-time course,—the more's the pity. The results do not often come as scientific discoveries. They are personal, rather; more after the manner of revelations,—data that the professors have little faith in. For the scientist cannot put an April dawn into a bottle, cannot cabin a Hockomock marsh, nor cage a December storm in a laboratory. And when, in such a place, did a scientist ever overturn a "wee bit heap o' weeds an' stibble"? Yet it is out of dawns and marshes and storms that the revelations come; yes, and out of mice nests, too, if you love all the out-of-doors, and chance to be ploughing late in the fall.

But there is the trouble with my professor. He never ploughs at all. How can he understand and believe? And isn't this the trouble with many of our preacher poets, also? Some of them spend their summers in the garden; but the true poet—and the naturalist—must stay later, and they must plough, plough the very edge of winter, if they would turn up what Burns did that November day in the field at Mossgiel.

How amazingly fortunate were the conditions of Burns's life! What if he had been professor of English literature at Edinburgh University? He might have written a life of Milton in six volumes,—a monumental work, but how unimportant compared with the lines "To a Mouse"!

We are going to live real life and write real poetry again,—when all who want to live, who want to write, draw directly upon life's first sources. To live simply, and out of the soil! To live by one's own ploughing, and to write!

Instead, how do we live? How do I live? Nine months in the year by talking bravely about books that I have not written. Between times I live on the farm, hoe, and think, and write,—whenever the hoeing is done. And where is my poem to a mouse?

Its silly wa's the win's are strewin!

With a whole farm o' foggage green, and all the year before me, I am not sure that I could build a single line of genuine poetry. But I am certain that, in living close to the fields, we are close to the source of true and great poetry, where each of us, at times, hears lines that Burns and Wordsworth left unmeasured,—lines that we at least may *live* into song.

Now, I have done just what my biological friend knew I would do,—made over my course of nature-study into a pleasant but idle waiting for inspiration. I have frankly turned poet! No, not unless Gilbert White and Jefferies, Thoreau, Burroughs, Gibson, Torrey, and Rowland Robinson are poets. But they are poets. We all are,—even the biologist, with half a chance,—and in some form we are all waiting for inspiration. The nature-lover who lives with his fields and skies simply puts himself in the way of the most and gentlest of such inspirations.

He may be ploughing when the spirit comes, or wandering, a mere boy, along the silent shores of a lake, and hooting at the owls. You remember the boy along the waters of Winander, how he would hoot at the owls in the twilight, and they would call back to him across the echoing lake? And when there would come a pause of baffling silence,

> Then, sometimes, in that silence, while he hung
> Listening, a gentle shock of mild surprise
> Has carried far into his heart the voice
> Of mountain-torrents; or the visible scene
> Would enter unawares into his mind
> With all its solemn imagery.

That is an inspiration, the kind of experience one has in living with the out-of-doors. It doesn't come from books, from laboratories, not even from an occasional tramp afield. It is out of companionship with nature that it comes; not often, perhaps, to any one, nor only to poets who write. I have had such experiences, such moments of quiet insight and uplift, while in the very narrowest of the paths of the woods.

It was in the latter end of December, upon a gloomy day that was heavy with the oppression of a coming storm. In the heart of the maple swamp all was still and cold and dead. Suddenly, as out of a tomb, I heard the small, thin cry of a tiny tree frog. And how small and thin it sounded in the vast silences of that winter swamp! And yet how clear and ringing! A thrill of life tingling out through the numb, nerveless body of the woods that has ever since made a dead day for me impossible.

That was an inspiration. I learned something, something deep and beautiful. Had I been Burns or Wordsworth I should have written a poem to Hyla. All prose as I am, I was, nevertheless, so quickened by that brave little voice as to write:—

The fields are bleak, the forests bare,
  The swirling snowflakes fall
About the trees a winding-sheet,
  Across the fields a pall.

A wide, dead waste, and leaden sky,
  Wild winds, and dark and cold!
The river's tongue is frozen thick,
  With life's sweet tale half told.

Dead! Ah, no! the white fields sleep,
  The frozen rivers flow;
And summer's myriad seed-hearts beat
  Within this breast of snow.

With spring's first green the holly glows
  And flame of autumn late,—
The embers of the summer warm
  In winter's roaring grate.

The thrush's song is silent now,
  The rill no longer sings,
But loud and long the strong winds strike
  Ten million singing strings.

O'er mountains high, o'er prairies far,
  Hark! the wild pæan's roll!
The lyre is strung 'twixt ocean shores
  And swept from pole to pole!

My meeting with that frog in the dead of winter was no trifling experience, nor one that the biologist ought to fail to understand. Had I been a poet, that meeting would have been of consequence to all the world; as I was, however, it meant something only to me,—a new point of view, an inspiration,— a beautiful poem that I cannot write.

This attitude of the nature-lover, because it is contemplative and poetical, is not therefore mystical or purely sentimental. Hooting at the owls and hearing things in baffling silences may not be scientific. Neither is it unscientific. The attitude of the boy beside the starlit lake is not that of Charlie, the man who helps me occasionally on the farm.

We were clearing up a bit of mucky meadow recently when we found a stone just above the surface that was too large for the horse to haul out. We decided to bury it.

Charlie took the shovel and mined away under the rock until he struck a layer of rather hard sandstone. He picked a while at this, then stopped a while; picked again, rather feebly, then stopped and began to think about it. It was hard work,—the thinking, I mean, harder than the picking,—but Charlie, however unscientific, is an honest workman, so he thought it through.

"Well," he said finally, "'t ain't no use, nohow. You can't keep it down. You bury the darned thing, and it'll come right up. I suppose it grows. Of course it does. It must. Everything grows."

Now that is an unscientific attitude. But that is not the mind of the nature-lover, of the boy with the baffling silences along the starlit lake. He is sentimental, certainly, yet not ignorant, nor merely vapid. He does not always wander along the lake by night. He is a nature-student, as well as a nature-lover, and he does a great deal more than hoot at the owls. This, though, is as near as he comes to anything scientific, and so worth while, according to the professor.

II

And it is as near as he ought to come to reality and facts—according to the philosopher.

"We want only the facts of nature," says the scientist. "Nothing in nature is worth while," says the philosopher, "but mood, background, atmosphere."

"Nor can I recollect that my mind," says one of our philosophers, "in these walks, was much called away from contemplation by the petty curiosities of the herbalist or birdlorist, for I am not one zealously addicted to scrutinizing into the minuter secrets of nature. It never seemed to me that a flower was made sweeter by knowing the construction of its ovaries.... The wood thrush and the veery sing as melodiously to the uninformed as to the subtly curious. Indeed, I sometimes think a little ignorance is wholesome in our communion with nature."

So it is. Certainly if ignorance, a great deal of ignorance, were unwholesome, then nature-study would be a very unhealthy course, indeed. For, when the most curious of the herbalists and birdlorists (Mr. Burroughs, say) has made his last prying peep into the private life of a ten-acre woodlot, he will still be wholesomely ignorant of the ways of nature. Is the horizon just back of the brook that marks the terminus of our philosopher's path? Let him leap across, walk on, on, out of his woods to the grassy knoll in the next pasture, and there look! Lo! far yonder the horizon! beyond a vaster forest than he has known, behind a range of higher rolling hills, within a shroud of wider, deeper mystery.

There isn't the slightest danger of walking off the earth; nor of unlearning our modicum of wholesome ignorance concerning the universe. The nature-lover may turn nature-student and have no fear of losing nature. The vision will not fade.

Let him go softly through the May twilight and wait at the edge of the swamp. A voice serene and pure, a hymn, a prayer, fills all the dusk with peace. Let him watch and see the singer, a brown-winged wood thrush, with full, spotted breast. Let him be glad that it is not a white-winged spirit, or a disembodied voice. And let him wonder the more that so plain a singer knows so divine a song.

Our philosopher mistakes his own dominant mood for the constant mood of nature. But nature has no constant mood. No more have we. Dawn and dusk are different moods. The roll of the prairie is unlike the temper of a winding cowpath in a New England pasture. Nature is not always sublime, awful, and mysterious; and no one but a philosopher is persistently contemplative. Indeed, at four o'clock on a June morning in some old apple orchard, even the philosopher would shout,—

"Hence, loathèd melancholy!"

He is in no mind for meditation; and it is just possible, before the day is done, that the capture of a drifting seed of the dandelion and the study of its fairy wings might so add to the wonder, if not to the sweetness, of the flower, as to give him thought for a sermon.

There are times when the companionship of your library is enough; there are other times when you want a single book, a chapter, a particular poem. It is good at times just to know that you are turning with the earth under the blue of the sky; and just as good again to puzzle over the size of the spots in the breasts of our several thrushes. For I believe you can hear more in the song when you know it is the veery and not the wood thrush singing. Indeed, I am acquainted with persons who had lived neighbors to the veery since childhood, and never had heard its song until the bird was pointed out to them. Then they could not help but hear.

No amount of familiarity will breed contempt for your fields. Is the summer's longest, brightest day long enough and bright enough, to dispel the brooding mystery of the briefest of its nights? And tell me, what of the vastness and terror of the sea will the deep dredges ever bring to the surface, or all the circumnavigating drive to shore? The nature-lover is a man in a particular mood; the nature-student is the same man in another mood, as the fading shadows of the morning are the same that lengthen and deepen in the afternoon. There are times when he will go apart into the desert places to pray. Most of the time, however, he will live contentedly within sound of the dinner horn, glad of the companionship of his bluebirds, chipmunks, and pine trees.

This is best. And the question most frequently asked me is, How can I come by a real love for my pine trees, chipmunks, and bluebirds? How can I know real companionship with nature?

How did the boy along the starlit lake come by it,—a companionship so real and intimate that the very cliffs knew him, that the owls answered him, that even the silences spoke to him, and the imagery of his rocks and skies became a part of the inner world in which he dwelt? Simply by living along Winander and hallooing so often to the owls that they learned to halloo in reply. You may need to be born again before you can talk the language of the owls; but if there is in you any hankering for the soil, then all you need for companionship with nature is a Winander of your own, a range, a haunt, that you can visit, walk around, and get home from in a day's time. If this region can be the pastures, woodlots, and meadows that make your own door-yard, then that is good; especially if you buy the land and live on it, for then Nature knows that you are not making believe. She will accept you as she does the peas you plant, and she will cherish you as she does them. This farm, or haunt, or range, you will come to know intimately: its flowers, birds, walls, streams, trees,—its features large and small, as they appear in June, and as they look in July and in January.

For the first you will need the how-to-know books,—these while you are getting acquainted; but soon acquaintance grows into friendship. You are done naming things. The meanings of things now begin to come home to you. Nature is taking you slowly back to herself. Companionship has begun.

Many persons of the right mind never know this friendship, because they never realize the necessity of being friendly. They walk through a field as they walk through a crowded street; they go into the country as they go abroad. And the result is that all this talk of the herbalist and birdlorist, to quote the philosopher again, seems "little better than cant and self-deception."

But let the philosopher cease philosophizing (he was also a hermit), and leave off hermiting; let him live at home with his wife and children, like the rest of us; let him work in the city for his living, hoe in his garden for his recreation; and then (I don't care by what prompting) let him study the lay of his neighbor fields, woods, and orchards until he knows every bird and beast, every tree-hole, earth-hole, even the times and places of the things that grow in the ground; let him do this through the seasons of the year,—for two or three years,—and he will know how to enjoy a woodchuck; he will understand many of the family affairs of his chipmunks; he will recognize and welcome back his bluebirds; he will love and often listen to the solemn talk of his pines.

V

Chickadee

Once (it was a good while ago, when I was a boy), I tried to write a poem. The first stanza ran:—

> I heard him when the reeds were young
> > Along a clover sea;
> Above the purple waves he hung,
> And o'er the fragrant waters flung
> > His storm of ecstasy;

and the last stanza ran:—

> He's left the meadows burnt and hot,
> > He's left me lone and drear;
> But still within the white-birch lot
> Cheeps Chickadee—whom I forgot
> > While Bobolink was here;

which means in plainer prose that chickadee does not sing a while in June and then fly away and leave us. He stays the year around; he is constant and faithful in his friendship, though I sometimes forget.

He cannot sing with bobolink. But suppose I could have only one of the birds? As it is, I get along for more than half the year without bobolink, but what would my out-of-doors be without chickadee? There is not a single day in the year that I cannot find him, no matter how hot, or cold, how hard it rains or snows. Often he is the only voice in all the silent woods, the only spark of life aglow in all my frozen winter world.

I was crunching along through the January dusk toward home. The cold was bitter. A half-starved partridge had just risen from the road and fluttered off among the naked bushes,—a moment of sound, a bit of life vanishing in the winter night of the woods. I knew the very hemlock in which he would roost; but what were the thick, snow-bent boughs of his hemlock, and what were all his winter feathers in such a night as this?—this vast of sweeping winds and frozen snow!

The road dipped from the woods into a meadow, where the winds were free. The cold was driving, numbing here with a power for death that the thermometer could not mark. I backed into the wind and hastened on toward the double line of elms that arched the road in front of the house. Already I could hear them creak and rattle like things of glass. It was not the sound of life. Nothing was alive; for what could live in this long darkness and fearful cold?

Could live? The question was hardly thought, when an answer was whirled past me into the nearest of the naked elms. A chickadee! He caught for an instant on a dead limb over the road, scrambled along to its broken tip, and whisked over into a hole that ran straight down the centre of the stub, down, for I don't know how far.

I stopped. The stub lay out upon the wind, with only an eddy of the gale sucking at the little round hole in the broken end, while far down in its hollow heart, huddling himself into a downy, dozy ball for the night, was the chickadee. I know by the very way he struck the limb and turned in that he had been there before. He knew whither, across the sweeping meadows, he was being blown. He had even helped the winds as they whirled him, for he had tarried along the roads till late. But he was safe for the night now, in the very bed, it may be, where he was hatched last summer, and where at this moment, who knows, were half a dozen other chickadees, the rest of that last summer's brood, unscathed still, and still sharing the old home hollow, as snug and warm this bitter night as in the soft May days when they were nestlings here together.

The cold drove me on; but the chickadee had warmed me and all my naked world of night and death. And so he ever does. The winter has yet to be that drives him seeking shelter to the south. I never knew it colder than in January and February of 1904. During both of those months, morning and evening, I drove through a long mile of empty, snow-buried woods. For days at a time I would not see even a crow, but morning and evening, at a certain dip in the road, two chickadees would fly from bush to bush across the hollow and cheer me on the way. They came out to the road, really, to pick up whatever scanty crumbs were to be found in my wake. They came also to hear me, to see me pass,—to escape for a moment, I think, the silence, desertion, and death of the woods. They helped me to escape, too.

Four other chickadees, all winter long, ate with us, sharing, as far as the double windows would allow, the cheer of our dining-room. We served them on the lilac bush outside the window, tying their suet on so that they could see us and we them during meal time. Perhaps it was mere suet, no feast of soul at all, that they got; but constantly, when our pie was opened, the birds began to sing,—a dainty dish indeed, savory, wholesome, and good for our souls.

There are states in the far Northwest where the porcupine is protected by law, as a last food resource for men lost and starving in the forests. Perhaps the porcupine was not designed by nature for any such purpose. Perhaps chickadee was not left behind by summer to feed our lost and starving hope through the cheerless months. But that is the use I make of him. He is summer's pledge to me. The woods are hollow, the winds chill, the earth cold and stiff, but there flits chickadee, and—I cannot lose faith, nor feel that this procession of bleak white days is all a funeral!

He is the only bird in my little world that I can find without fail three hundred and sixty-five days in the year. From December to the end of March he comes daily to my lilac bush for suet; from April to early July he is busy with domestic cares in the gray birches of the woodlot; from August to December he and his family come hunting quietly and sociably as a little flock among the trees and bushes of the farm; and from then on he is back for his winter meals at "The Lilac."

Is it any wonder that he was the first bird I ever felt personally acquainted with, and the first bird my children knew? That early acquaintance, however, was not due to his abundance and intrusion, as it might be with the English sparrow, but rather due to the cheerful, confiding, sociable spirit of the little bird. He drops down and peeps under your hat-brim to see what manner of boy you are, and if you are really fit to be abroad in this world, so altogether good—for chickadees.

He has a mission to perform besides the eating of eggs and grubs of the pestiferous insects. This destruction he does that the balance of things may be maintained out of doors. He has quite another work to do, which is not economic, and which, in nowise, is a matter of fine feathers or sweet voice, but simply a matter of sweet nature, vigor, and concentrated cheerfulness.

I said he is summer's pledge, the token of hope to me. He is a lesson also. I don't often find sermons in stones, because, no doubt, I look so little for the sermons, so little for the very stones. But I cannot help seeing chickadee,—and chickadee is all sermon. I hear him on a joyous May morning calling *Chick-a-dee! dee! Chick-a-dee! dee!*—brisk, bright, and cheery; or, soft and gentle as a caress, he whistles, *Phœ-ee-bee! Phœ-ee-bee!* I meet him again on the edge of a bleak, midwinter night. He is hungry and cold, and he calls, as I hasten along, *Chick-a-dee! dee! Chick-a-dee! dee!*—brisk, bright, and cheery; or, soft and gentle as a caress, he whistles, *Phœ-ee-bee! Phœ-ee-bee!*

Will you lend me your wings, chickadee, those invisible wings on which you ride the winds of life so evenly? For I would hang my ill-balanced soul between them, as your bird soul hangs, and fly as you fly.

The abundant summer, the lean and wolfish winter, find chickadee cheerful and gentle. He is busier at some seasons than at others, with fewer chances for friendship. He almost disappears in the early summer. But this is because of family cares; and because the bigger, louder birds have come back, and the big leaves have come out and hidden him. A little searching, and you will discover him, in one of your old decayed fence posts, maybe, or else deep in the swamp, foraging for a family so numerous that they spill over at the door of their home.

Here about the farm, this is sure to be a gray birch home. Other trees will do—on a pinch. I have found chickadee nesting in live white oaks, maples, upturned roots, and tumbling fence posts. These were shifts, however, mere houses, not real homes. The only good homelike trees are old gray birches dead these many years and gone to punk,—mere shells of tough circular bark walls.

Why has chickadee this very decided preference? Is it a case of protective coloration,—the little gray and black bird choosing to nest in this little gray and black tree because bird and tree so exactly match each other in size and color? Or (and there are many instances in nature) is there a subtle strain of poetry in chickadee's soul, something æsthetic, that leads him into this exquisite harmony,—into this little gray house for his little gray self?

Explain it as you may, it is a fact that this little bird shows a marked preference, makes deliberate choice, and in his choice is protection, and poetry, too. Doubtless he follows the guidance of a sure and watchful instinct (whatever instinct be), but who shall deny to him a share of the higher, finer things of the imagination? a share of real æsthetic taste?

His life inside the birch is of a piece with the artistic exterior. It is all gentle and sweet and idyllic. There is no happier spot in the summer woods than that about the birch of the chickadees; and none whose happiness you will be so little liable to disturb.

Before the woods were in leaf one spring I found a pair of

chickadees building in a birch along the edge of the swamp. They had just begun, having dug out only an inch of cavity. It was very interesting to discover them doing the work themselves, for usually they refit some abandoned chamber or adapt a ready-made hole.

The birch was a long, limbless cylinder of bark, broken off about fourteen feet up, and utterly rotten, the mere skin of a tree stuffed with dust. I could push my finger into it at any point. It was so weak that every time the birds lighted upon the top the whole stub wobbled and reeled. Surely they were building their house upon the sand. Any creature without wings would have known that. Birds, however, seem to have lost the sense of such insecurity, often placing their nests as if they expected them also to take wings and fly to safety when the rains descend and the winds come.

This shaking stub of the chickadees was standing directly beneath a great overshadowing pine, where, if no partridge bumped into it, if two squirrels did not scamper up it together, if the crows nesting overhead did not discover it, if no strong wind bore down upon it from the meadow side, it might totter out the nesting season. But it didn't. The birds were leaving too much to luck. I knew it, and should have pushed their card house down, then and there, and saved the greater ruin later. Perhaps so, but I was too interested in their labor.

Both birds were working when I discovered them, and so busily that my coming up did not delay them for a single billful. It was not hard digging, but it was very slow, for chickadee is neither carpenter nor mason. He has difficulty in killing a hard-backed beetle. So, whenever you find him occupying a clean-walled cavity, with a neat, freshly clipped doorway, you may be sure that some woodpecker built the house, not this

short-billed, soft-tailed little tit. He lacks both the bill-chisel
and the tail-brace. Perhaps the explanation of his fondness for
birch trees lies here: they die young and soon decay.

The birds were going down through the top, not by a hole
in the leathery rind of the sides, for the bark would have been
too tough for their beaks. They would drop into the top of
the stub, pick up a wad of decayed wood, and fly off to the
dead limb of the pine. Here, with a jerk and a snap of their
bills, they would scatter the stuff in a shower so thin and far
around that I could neither hear it fall nor find a trace of it
upon the dead leaves of the ground. This nest would never
be betrayed by the workmen's chips.

Between the pair there averaged three beakfuls of excavat-
ing every two minutes, one of the birds regularly shoveling
twice to the other's once. They looked so exactly alike that I
could not tell which bird was pushing the enterprise; but I
have my suspicions.

There is nothing so superior about his voice or appearance
that he should thus shirk. He was doing part of his duty,
apparently, but it was half-hearted work. Hers was the real
interest, the real anxiety; and hers the initiative. To be a male
and show off! That's the thing. To be a male and let your wife
carry the baby! The final distinctive difference between a truly
humanized, civilized man and all other males of every order,
is a willingness to push the baby carriage.

The finer the feathers or the song among male birds the less
use they are in practical, domestic ways. Fine beaux, captivat-
ing lovers, they become little else than a nuisance as husbands.
One of my friends has been watching a pair of bluebirds
building. The male sat around for a week without bringing
in a feather. Then one day he was seen to enter the hole, after

his busy mate had just left it, and carry out a beakful of grass which he scattered to the winds in pure perversity, criticising her bungling work, maybe! More likely he was jealous.

Chickadee was no such precious fool as that. He was doing something; trying to drown his regret for the departing honeymoon in hard labor, not, however, to the danger of his health.

I sat a long time watching the work. It went on in perfect silence, not a chirp, not the sound of a fluttering wing. The swamp along whose margin the birds were building had not a joyous atmosphere. Damp, dim-shadowed, and secret, it seemed to have laid its spell upon the birds. Their very gray and black was as if mixed of the dusk, and of the gray, half-light of the swamp; their noiseless coming and going was like the slipping to and fro of shadows. They were a part of it all, and that sharing was their defense, the best defense they knew.

It didn't save their nest, however. They felt and obeyed the spirit of the swamp in their own conduct, but the swamp did not tell them where to build. It was about three weeks later that I stopped again under the pine and found the birch stub in pieces upon the ground. Some robber had been after the eggs and had brought the whole house tumbling down. This is not the fate of all such birch-bark houses. Now and again they escape; but it is always a matter for wonder.

I was following an old disused wood road once when I scared a robin from her nest. Her mate joined her, and together they raised a great hubbub. Immediately a chewink, a pair of vireos, and two black and white warblers joined the robins in their din. Then a chickadee appeared. He (I say "he" knowingly; and here he quite redeems himself) had a worm in his beak. His anxiety seemed so real that I began to watch him, when, looking down among the stones for a place to step, what should I see but his mate emerging from the end of a birch stump at my very feet. She had heard the din and had come out to see what it was all about. At sight of her, he hastened with his worm, brushing my face, almost, as he darted to her side. She took it sweetly, for she knew he had intended it for her. But how do I know that? Perhaps he meant it for the young! There were no young in the nest, only eight eggs. Even after the young came (there were eight of them!), and when life, from daylight to dark, was one ceaseless, hurried hunt for worms, I saw him over and over again fly to her side caressingly and tempt her to eat.

The house of this pair did not fall. How could it when it stood precisely two and a half feet from the ground! But that it wasn't looted is due to the sheer audacity of its situation. It stood alone, against the road, so close that the hub of a low wheel in passing might have knocked it down. Perhaps a hundred persons had brushed it in going by. How many dogs and cats had overlooked it no one can say, nor how many skunks and snakes and squirrels. The accident that discovered it to me happened apparently to no one else, and I was friendly.

Cutting a tiny window in the bark just above the eggs, I looked in upon the little people every day. I watched them grow and fill the cavity and hang over at the top. I was there the day they forced my window open, the day when there was no more room at the top, and when, at the call of their parents, one after another of this largest and sweetest of bird families found his wings and flew away through the woods.

VI

The Missing Tooth

THE snow had melted from the river meadows, leaving them flattened, faded, and stained with mud,—a dull, dreary waste in the gray February. I had stopped beside a tiny bundle of bones that lay in the matted grass a dozen feet from a ditch. Here, still showing, was the narrow path along which the bones had dragged themselves; there the hole by which they had left the burrow in the bank of the ditch. They had crawled out in this old runway, then turned off a little into the heavy autumn grass and laid them down. The rains had come and the winter snows. The spring was breaking now, and the small bundle, gently loosened and uncovered, was whitening on the wide, bare meadow.

I had recognized the bones at once as the skeleton of a muskrat. It was something peculiar in the way they lay that had caused me to pause. They seemed outstretched, as if composed by gentle hands, the hands of Sleep. They had not been flung down. The delicate ribs had fallen in, but not a bone was broken or displaced, not one showed the splinter of shot, or the crack that might have been made by a steel trap. No violence had been done them. They had been touched by nothing rougher than the snow. Out into the hidden runway they had crept. Death had passed them here; but no one else in all the winter months.

The creature had died—a "natural" death. It had starved, while a hundred acres of plenty lay round about. Picking up the skull, I found the jaws locked together as if they were a single solid bone. One of the two incisor teeth of the upper jaw was missing, and apparently had never developed. The opposite tooth on the lower jaw, thus unopposed and so unworn, had grown beyond its normal height up into the empty socket above, then on, turning outward and piercing the cheek-bone in front of the eye, whence, curving like a boar's tusk, it had slowly closed the jaws and locked them, rigid, set, as fixed as jaws of stone.

Death had lingered cruelly. At first the animal had been able to gnaw; but as the tooth curved through the bones of the face and gradually tightened the jaws, the creature got less and less to eat, until, one day, creeping out of the burrow for food, the poor wretch was unable to get back.

One seldom comes upon the like of this. It is commoner than we think; but it is usually hidden away and quickly over. How often do we see a wild thing sick,—a bird or animal suffering from an accident, or dying, like this muskrat, because of some physical defect? The struggle between two lives for life—the falling of the weak as prey to the strong—is ever before us; but this single-handed fight between the creature and Nature is a far rarer, silenter tragedy. Nature is too swift, too merciless to allow us time for sympathy. It was she who taught the old Roman to take away his weak and malformed offspring and expose it on the hills.

There is, at best, scarcely a fighting chance in the meadow. Only strength and craft may win. The muskrat with the missing tooth never enters the race at all. He slinks from some abandoned burrow, and, if the owl and mink are not watching, dies alone in the grass, and we rarely know.

I shall never forget the impression made upon me by those quiet bones. It was like that made by my first visit to a great city hospital,—out of the busy, cheerful street into a surgical ward, where the sick and injured lay in long white lines. We tramp the woods and meadows and never step from the sweet air and the pure sunlight of health into a hospital. But that is not because no sick, ill-formed, or injured are there. The proportion is smaller than among us humans, and for very good reasons, yet there is much real suffering, and to come upon it, as we will, now and then, must certainly quicken our understanding and deepen our sympathy with the life out of doors.

No sensible person could for a moment believe the animals capable of suffering as a human being can suffer, or that there is any such call for our sympathy from them as from our human neighbors. But an unselfish sharing of the life of the fields demands that we take part in all of it,—and all of it is but little short of tragedy. Nature wears a brave face. Her smile is ever in the open, her laughter quick and contagious. This brave front is no mask. It is real. Sunlight, song, color, form, and fragrance are real. And so our love and joy in Nature is real. Real, also, should be our love and sorrow with Nature. For do I share fully in as much of her life as even the crow lives as long as I think of the creature only with admiration for his cunning or with wrath for his destruction of my melons and corn?

A crow has his solemn moments. He frequently knows fear, pain, hunger, accident, and disease; he knows something very like affection and love. For all that, he is a mere crow. But a mere crow is no mean thing. Few of us, indeed, are ourselves, and as much besides as a mere crow. A real love, however, will give us part in all of his existence. We will forage and fight with him; we will parley and play; and when the keen north winds find him in the frozen pines, we will suffer, too.

With Nature as mere waters, fields, and skies, it is, perhaps, impossible for us to sorrow. She is too self-sufficient, too impersonal. She asks, or compels, everything except tears. But when she becomes birds and beasts,—a little world of individuals among whom you are only one of a different kind,—then all the others, no matter their kind, are earth-born companions and fellow mortals.

Here are the meadow voles. I know that my hay crop is shorter every year for them,—a very little shorter. And I can look with satisfaction at a cat carrying a big bobtailed vole out of my mowing. The voles are rated, along with other mice, as injurious to man. I have an impulse to plant both of my precious feet upon every one that stirs in its runway.

If that feeling was habitual once, it is so no longer; for now it is only when the instincts of the farmer get the better of me that I spring at this quiet stir in the grass. Perhaps, long ago, my forbears wore claws, like pussy; and, perhaps (there isn't the slightest doubt), I should develop claws if I continued to jump at every mouse in the grass because he is a mouse, and because I have a little patch of mucky land in hay.

One day I came upon two of my voles struggling in the

water. They were exhausted and well-nigh dead. I helped them out as I should have helped out any other creature, and having saved them, why, what could I do but let them go—even into my own meadow? This has happened several times.

When the drought dries the meadow, the voles come to the deep, walled spring at the upper end, apparently to drink. The water usually trickles over the curb, but in a long dry spell it shrinks a foot or more below the edge, and the voles, once within for their drink, cannot get out. Time and time again I had fished them up, until I thought to leave a board slanting down to the water, so that they could climb back to the top.

It is stupid and careless to drown thus. The voles are blunderers. White-footed mice and house mice are abundant in the stumps and grass of the vicinity, but they never tumble into the spring. Still, I am partly responsible for the voles, for I walled up the spring and changed it into this trap. I owe them the drink and the plank, for certainly there are rights of mice, as well as of men, in this meadow of mine, where I do little but mow. But even if they have no rights, surely

> A daimen icker in a thrave
> 'S a sma' request

for such of them as the foxes, cats, skunks, snakes, hawks, and owls leave! Rights or no, hay or no, I don't jump at *my* meadow mice any more, for fear of killing one who has taken a cup of cold water from me off the plank, or has had my helping hand out of the depths of the spring.

It is wholesome to be the good Samaritan to a meadow mouse, to pour out, even waste, a little of the oil and wine of sympathy on the humblest of our needy neighbors.

Here are the chimney swallows. One can look with complacency, with gratitude, indeed, upon the swallows of other chimneys, as they hawk in the sky; yet, when the little creatures, so useful, but so uncombed and unfumigated, set up their establishments in *your* chimney, to the jeopardy of the whole house, then you need an experience like mine.

I had had a like experience years before, when the house did not belong to me. Now, however, the house was mine, and if it became infested because of the swallows, I could not move away; so I felt like burning them in the chimney, bag and baggage. There were four nests, as nearly as I could make out, and, from the frequent squeakings, I knew they were all filled with young. Then one day, when the birds were feathered and nearly ready to fly, there came a rain that ran wet far down the sooty chimney, loosened the mortar of the nests, and sent them crashing into the fireplace.

Some of the young birds were killed outright; the others were at my mercy, flung upon me,—helpless, wailing infants! Of course I made it comfortable for them on the back-log, and let their mothers flutter down unhindered to feed them. Had I understood the trick, I would have hawked for them and helped feed them myself.

They made a great thunder in the chimney; they rattled down into the living-room a little soot; but nothing further came of it. We were not quarantined. On the contrary, we had our reward, according to promise; for it was an extremely interesting event to us all. It dispelled some silly qualms, it gave us intimate part in a strange small life, so foreign, yet so closely linked to our own, and it made us pause with wonder that even our empty, sooty chimney could be made use of by Nature to our great benefit.

I wonder if the nests of the chimney swallows came tumbling down when the birds used to build in caves and hollow trees? It is a most extraordinary change, this change from the trees to the chimneys, and it does not seem to have been accompanied by an increase of architectural wisdom necessary to meet all the contingencies of the new hollow. The mortar or glue, which, I imagine, held firmly in the empty trees, will not mix with the chimney soot, so that the nest, especially when crowded with young, is easily loosened by the rain, and is sometimes even broken away by the slight wing-stroke of a descending swallow, or by the added weight of a parent bird as it settles with food.

We little realize how frequent fear is among the birds and animals, nor how often it proves fatal. A situation which would have caused no trouble ordinarily, becomes through sudden fright a tangle or a trap. I have known many a quail to bolt into a fast express train and fall dead. Last winter I left the large door of the barn open, so that my flock of juncos could feed inside upon the floor. They found their way into the hayloft, and went up and down freely. On two or three occasions I happened in so suddenly that they were thoroughly frightened, and flew madly into the cupola to escape through the windows. They beat against the glass until utterly dazed, and would have perished there, had I not climbed up later and brought them down. So thousands of the migrating birds perish yearly by flying wildly against the dazzling lanterns of the lighthouses, and thousands more lose their way in the thick darkness of the stormy nights, or are blown out of their course, and drift away to sea.

Hasty, careless, miscalculated movements are not as frequent among the careful wild folk as among us, perhaps; but there is abundant evidence of their occasional occurrence and of their sometimes fatal results.

Several instances are recorded of birds that have been tangled in the threads of their nests; and one case of a bluebird that was caught in the flying meshes of an oriole's nest into which it had been spying.

I once found the mummied body of a chippy twisting and swinging in the leafless branches of a peach tree. The little creature was suspended in a web of horsehair about two inches below the nest. It looked as if she had brought a snarled bunch of the hair and left it loose in the twigs. Later on, a careless step and her foot was fast, when every frantic effort for freedom only tangled her the worse. In the nest above were four other tiny mummies,—a double tragedy that might with care have been averted.

A similar fate befell a song sparrow that I discovered hanging dead upon a barbed-wire fence. By some chance it had slipped a foot through an open place between the two twisted strands, and then, fluttering along, had wedged the leg and broken it in the struggle to escape.

We have all held our breath at the hazardous traveling of the squirrels in the treetops. What other animals take such risks,—leaping at dizzy heights from bending limbs to catch the tips of limbs still smaller, saving themselves again and again by the merest chance.

But luck sometimes fails. My brother, a careful watcher in the woods, was hunting on one occasion, when he saw a gray squirrel miss its footing in a tree and fall, breaking its neck upon a log beneath.

I have frequently known them to fall short distances, and once I saw a red squirrel come to grief like the gray squirrel above. He was scurrying through the tops of some lofty pitch pines, a little hurried and flustered at sight of me, and nearing the end of a high branch was in the act of springing, when the dead tip cracked under him and he came tumbling head-long. The height must have been forty feet, so that before he reached the ground he had righted himself,—his tail out and legs spread,—but the fall was too great. He hit the earth with a dull thud, and before I could reach him lay dead upon the needles, with blood oozing from his eyes and nostrils.

Unhoused and often unsheltered, the wild things suffer as we hardly yet understand. No one can estimate the deaths of a year from severe cold, heavy storms, high winds and tides. I have known the nests of a whole colony of gulls and terns to be swept away in a great storm; and I have seen the tides, over and over, flood the inlet marshes, and drown out the nests in the grass,—those of the clapper-rails by thousands.

I remember a late spring storm that came with the return-ing redstarts and, in my neighborhood, killed many of them. Toward evening of that day one of the little black and orange voyageurs fluttered against the window and we let him in, wet, chilled, and so exhausted that for a moment he lay on his back in my open palm. Soon after there was another soft tapping at the window,—and two little redstarts were sharing our cheer and drying their butterfly wings in our warmth.

During the summer of 1903 one of the commonest of the bird calls about the farm was the whistle of the quails. A covey roosted down the hillside within fifty yards of the house. Then came the winter,—such a winter as the birds had never known. Since then, just once have we heard the whistle of a quail, and that, perhaps, was the call of one which a game protective association had liberated in the woods about two miles away.

The birds and animals are not as weather-wise as we; they cannot foretell as far ahead nor provide as certainly against need, despite the popular notion to the contrary.

We point to the migrating birds, to the muskrat houses, and the hoards of the squirrels, and say, "How wise and far-sighted these nature-taught children are!" True, they are, but only for conditions that are normal. Their wisdom does not cover the exceptional. The gray squirrels did not provide for the unusually hard weather of the winter of 1904. Three of them from the woodlot came begging of me, and lived on my wisdom, not on their own.

Consider the ravens, that neither sow nor reap, that have neither storehouse nor barn, yet they are fed,—but not always. Indeed, there are few of our winter birds that go hungry so often, and that die in so great numbers for lack of food and shelter, as the crows.

After severe and protracted cold, with a snow-covered ground, a crow-roost looks like a battlefield, so thick lie the dead and wounded. Morning after morning the flock goes over to forage in the frozen fields, and night after night returns hungrier, weaker, and less able to resist the cold. Now, as the darkness falls, a bitter wind breaks loose and sweeps down upon the pines.

> List'ning the doors an' winnocks rattle,
> I thought me on the owrie cattle,

and how often I have thought me on the crows biding the night yonder in the moaning pines! So often, as a boy, and with so real an awe, have I watched them returning at night, that the crows will never cease flying through my wintry sky,—an endless line of wavering black figures, weary, retreating figures, beating over in the early dusk.

To-night another wild storm sweeps across the January fields. All the afternoon the crows have been going over, and at five o'clock are still passing though the darkness settles rapidly. Now it is eight, and the long night is but just begun. The storm is increasing. The wind shrieks about the house, whirling the fine snow in hissing eddies past the corners and driving it on into long, curling crests across the fields. I can hear the roar as the wind strikes the shoal of pines where the fields roll into the woods,—a vast surf sound, but softer and higher, with a wail like the wail of some vast heart in pain.

I can see the tall trees rock and sway with their burden of dark forms. As close together as they can crowd on the bending limbs cling the crows, their breasts turned all to the storm. With crops empty and bodies weak, they rise and fall in the cutting, ice-filled wind for thirteen hours of night!

Is it a wonder that the life fires burn low? that the small flames flicker and go out?

VII

The Sign of the Shad-bush

THE shad-bush is open! My bees have seen the sign. They are dropping down upon the alighting-boards of their hives and running with little bags of gold into the still half-closed entrances. During the sunny hours of the last three weeks there has been a quiet buzzing about the hives: the bees have been visiting the early alders, the soft maples, and the dusty-catkined willows; but not before to-day, the first day of the blowing shad-bush, have things been busy at the hives,—have they hummed.

Off along the meadows I can see large patches of garnet against the purple of the sky,—the bloom of the red maples. As I approach, a soft murmur around and through the misty garnet fills the air, like the murmur of a million tiny tongues. Nearer still, and I can see the bees. Here is where they are getting their gold. But not all of it. Some of it to-day is coming from the marsh marigolds.

Early in April, before the shad-bush had opened, or a bee had ventured to the meadows, I picked the first hardy blossom of the marigolds out of icy water, out of mud that had barely thawed. A token this, a promise; but not the sure sign of spring. The bees did not see it; they were waiting, like me, for the shad-bush. So were the marigolds, for to-day the low, wet edge of the meadow ditch is all aglow with the shining of their gold, which the bees are pocketing by the thighful. Among the "flowers," the marigolds are the first here to offer a harvest for the hives.

The procession is under way. The assembling began weeks ago, with the March hepatica, the stray April arbutus, wind-flower, spice-bush, and bloodroot. There were saxifrage and everlasting out, too; but they all came singly and timidly. There was no movement of the flowers until the shad-bush opened. Now the marigolds appear in companies, the windflowers drift together, and the hepaticas, leading the line, make a show. The procession of the flowers has started; spring is here.

My spring, I should have said. Your spring came long ago, perhaps, or still delays. "The dandelion tells me when to look for the swallow, the dog-tooth violet when to expect the wood thrush, and when I have found the wake-robin in bloom I know the season is fairly inaugurated. With me this flower is associated, not merely with the awakening of Robin, for he has been awake some weeks, but with the universal awakening and rehabilitation of Nature."

I watch for the sign of the shad-bush. Spring! There is the smell of spring in the yellow spice-bush; the sound of spring in the trills of the hylas; the color of spring in the blue of the hepatica. A February rain spatters your face with spring; the wild geese trumpet spring in the gray skies as they pass; the bluebird brings spring in spite of your fears and the weather:—

All white and still lie stream and hill—
The winter cold and drear!
When from the skies, a bluebird flies
And—spring is here!

True enough. But then suddenly the bluebird disappears; a heavy snowstorm sets in (as happened not many springs ago), and thousands of the birds perish. Spring was here. It has gone again. And so it will come and go until the shad-bush blooms—for me.

You will not miss one of the returning birds, not even the wild geese; not one of the early flowers, either, by waiting for the shad-bush. The skunk-cabbage and pussy-willow are still in blossom; and still in the woods and fields is the smell of the soil,—that fragrance, that essence which is the breath of the wakening earth. You can yet taste it on the lips of the hepatica, the arbutus, and bloodroot. It still lingers on the early catkins, too,—a strangely rare and delicate odor, that is not of the flowers at all, but of the earth, and sweeter than any perfume that the summer can distill.

It has been a slow, unwilling season until to-day, so slow that the green still shows richest in the sheltered meadows, and the lively color on the rocky slope that runs up from my tiny river is largely the color of mosses and Christmas ferns. Here is a stretch of southern exposure, however, and here are spots where springtime came weeks ago. Already the dog-tooth violets are out in a sunny saucer between the rocks; just above them, on an unshaded shelf, is a patch of saxifrage, and close at hand among the clefts, their "honey pitcher upside down," swing the first of my columbines.

Yet Spring does not come thus by spots; she does not crawl

out and sun herself like a lizard. The columbine seeks the sun, but the hepaticas came up and opened their exquisite eyes in the deepest, dampest shadows of the woods. I have seen them and the lingering snowdrifts together. Many of them are never touched with a sunbeam, their warmth and life coming from within, from a store saved through the winter, rather than from without. Here under the mat of fallen leaves and winter snow they have kept enough of the summer to make a spring.

The fires of summer are never out. They are only banked in the winter, smouldering always under the snow, and quick to brighten and burst into blaze. There came a warm day in January, and across my thawing path crawled a woolly bear caterpillar, a vanessa butterfly flitted through the woods, and the juncos sang. That night a howling snowstorm swept out of the north. The coals were covered again. So they kindled and darkened, until to-day they leap from the ashes of winter, a pure, thin blaze in the shad-bush, to burn higher and hotter across the summer, to flicker and die away, a line of yellow embers in the weird witch-hazel of the autumn.

At the sign of the shad-bush the doors of my springtime swing wide open. My birds are back, my turtles are out, my squirrels and woodchucks show themselves, my garden is ready to plough and plant. There is not a stretch of wood-land or meadow now that shows a trace of winter. Over the pasture the bluets are beginning to drift, as if the haze, on the distant hills, floating down in the night, had been caught in the dew-wet grass. They wash the field to its borders in their delicate azure hue.

Along with the bluets ("innocence" we should always call them), under the open sky, there unroll in the wet shaded bottoms of the maple swamps the pointed arum leaves of the Jacks, or Indian turnips. How they fight for room! There are patches where all the pews are pulpits, with some of the preachers standing three deep.

Now why should there be such a scramble for place among the Jacks, while just above them in the dry woods the large showy lady's-slipper opens in isolated splendor? Here is one, yonder another, with room between for a thousand. Occasionally you will see a dozen together, though not in a crowd; but more often the solitary blossom opens alone and far removed from any of its kind.

The lady's-slippers, however, are really social compared with the arbutus. Here is a flower that is naturally tribal,—bound together by common root-stalks, trailing shrubby plants that seem free to possess the earth. They were doubtless here in the soil before the Pilgrim came. The angels planted them, I am sure, for they smell of a celestial garden. The paths of heaven are carpeted with them, not paved with gold. But something is the matter with this earthly soil. They grow just where they were originally planted and nowhere else. There was a patch set in the woods three quarters of a mile, as the crow flies, from my front door. That was several millenniums ago. It is there still, a patch as big as my hat. There are other scattered bits of it beyond, but none any nearer to me, yet the soil seems the same, and there are woods all the way between.

Were it as common as the violet, perhaps some of its sweetness would be lost upon us. After all, the heavenly streets may be paved with gold, and instead of a carpet of arbutus, we shall find patches of it only, hidden away under the fallen leaves of the Elysian groves. For we shall need to get out of even the celestial city into the open fields and woods, and I can think of nothing so likely to draw us away from our mansions and beyond the pearly gates as the chance to go "May-flowering."

And, even here below, among the unransomed souls of Boston, when Mayflower-time arrives, you may see young men and maidens, children and grandfathers, trooping out to the woods for a handful of the flowers. And up from the Cape, to those who cannot go into the woods, the flowers, themselves, come,—tight, naked bunches, stripped of all but the pink of their faces and the sweet of their souls. They possess every quarter of the city. Jew and Gentile sell them, Greek and Barbarian buy them, as they buy and sell no other wild flower.

Why, then, is it not the arbutus, instead of the shad-bush, that spells for me the spring? I don't know; unless it is because the shad-bush takes deeper hold upon my imagination. It certainly is not its form, or color, or fragrance,—though it has grace,—an airy, misty, half-substantial shape, a wraith in the leafless woods; it has odor, too, and color. But it is something more than all of these that the soft blowing shad-bush means to me. Perhaps the something is in its name,—because it links my inland round with the round of the sea; and because it links this present narrowing round with the wide-winging round of the past.

At the sign of the shad-bush I know the fish are running,— the sturgeon up the Delaware; the shad into Cohansey Creek; and through Five-Forks Sluice, these soft, stirring nights, I know the catfish are slipping. Is there any boy now in Lupton's Meadows to watch them come? to listen in the moonlit quiet for the *splash*, *splash*, as the fish pass up through the main ditch toward the dam?

At the sign of the shad-bush how swiftly the tides of life rise! how mysteriously their currents run! drifting, flying, flow-

ing, creeping—colors, perfumes, forms, and voices—across
the heavens, over the earth, and down the deep, dim aisles
of the sea! and down the deep, dim aisles of our memories.

VIII

The Nature Movement

I was hurrying across Boston Common. Two or three hundred others were hurrying with me. But ahead, at the union of several paths, was a crowd, standing still. I kept hurrying on, not to join the crowd, but simply to keep up the hurry. The crowd was not standing still, it was a-hurrying, too, scattering as fast as it gathered, and as it scattered I noticed that it wore a smile. I hastened up, pushed in, as I had done a score of times on the Common, and got my glimpse of the show. It was not a Mormon preaching, not a single-taxer, not a dog fight. It was Billy, a gray squirrel, taking peanuts out of a bootblack's pocket. And every age, sex, sort, and condition of Bostonian came around to watch the little beast shuck the nuts and bury them singly in the grass of the Common.

"Ain't he a cute little cuss, mister?" said the boy of the brush, feeling the bottom of his empty pocket, and looking up into the prosperous face of Calumet and Hecla at his side. C. and H. smiled, slipped something into the boy's hand with which to buy another pocketful of peanuts for Billy, and hurried down to State Street.

This crowd on the Common is nothing exceptional. It happens every day, and everywhere, the wide country over. We are all stopping to watch, to feed, and—to smile. The longest, most far-reaching pause in our hurrying American life to-day is this halt to look at the out-of-doors, this attempt to share its life; and nothing more significant is being added to our American character than the resulting thoughtfulness, sympathy, and simplicity,—the smile on the faces of the crowd hurrying over the Common.

Whether one will or not, he is caught up by this nature movement and set adrift in the fields. It may, indeed, be "adrift" for him until he gets thankfully back to the city. "It was a raw November day," wrote one of these new nature students, who happened also to be a college student, "and we went for our usual Saturday's birding into the woods. The chestnuts were ripe, and we gathered a peck between us. On our way home, we discovered a small bird perched upon a cedar tree with a worm in its beak. It was a hummingbird, and after a little searching we found its tiny nest close up against the trunk of the cedar, full of tiny nestlings just ready to fly."

This is what they find, many of these who are caught up by the movement toward the fields; but not all of them. A little five-year-old from the village came out to see me recently, and while playing in the orchard she brought me five flowers, called them by their right names, and told me how they grew. Down in the loneliest marshes of Delaware Bay I know a lighthouse keeper and his solitary neighbor, a farmer: both have been touched by this nature spirit; both are interested, informed, and observant. The farmer there, on the old Zane's Place, is no man of books, like the rector of Selborne, but he is a man of birds and beasts, of limitless marsh and bay and sky, of everlasting silence and wideness and largeness and eternal solitude. He could write a Natural History of the Maurice River Marshes.

These are not rare cases. The nature books, the nature magazines, the nature teachers, are directing us all to the out-of-doors. I subscribe to a farm journal (club rates, twenty-five cents a year!) in which an entire page is devoted to "nature studies," while the whole paper is remarkably fresh and odorous of the real fields. In the city, on my way to and from the station, I pass three large bookstores, and from March until July each of these shops has a big window given over almost continuously to "nature books." I have before me from one of these shops a little catalogue of nature books—"a select list"—for 1907, containing 233 titles, varying in kind all the way from "The Tramp's Handbook" to one (to a dozen) on the very stable subject of "The Farmstead." These are all distinctively "nature books," books with an appeal to sentiment as well as to sense, and very unlike the earlier desiccated, unimaginative treatises.

There are a multitude of other signs that show as clearly as the nature books how full and strong is this tide that sets toward the open fields and woods. There are as many and as good evidences, too, of the genuineness of this interest in the out-of-doors. It may be a fad just now to adopt abandoned farms, to attend parlor lectures on birds, and to possess a how-to-know library. It is pathetic to see "nature study" taught by schoolma'ams who never did and who never will climb a rail fence; it is sad, to speak softly, to have the makers of certain animal books preface the stories with a declaration of their absolute truth; it is passing sad that the unnatural natural history, the impossible out-of-doors, of some of the recent nature books, should have been created. But fibs and failures and impossibilities aside, there still remains the thing itself,—the widespread turning to nature, and the deep, vital need to turn.

The note of sincerity is clear, however, in most of our nature writers; the faith is real in most of our nature teachers; and the love,—who can doubt the love of the tens of thousands of those whose feet feel the earth nowadays, whose lives share in the existence of some pond or wood or field? And who can doubt the rest, the health, the sanity, and the satisfaction that these get from the companionship of their field or wood or pond?

There is no way of accounting for the movement that reflects in the least upon its reality and genuineness. It may be only the appropriation by the common people of the world that the scientists have discovered to us; it may be a popular reaction against the conventionality of the eighteenth century; or the result of our growing wealth and leisure; or a fashion set by Thoreau and Burroughs,—one or all of these may account for its origin; but nothing can explain the movement away, or hinder us from being borne by it out, at least a little way, under the open of heaven, to the great good of body and soul.

Among the cultural influences of our times that have developed the proportions of a movement, this so-called nature movement is peculiarly American. No such general, widespread turning to the out-of-doors is seen anywhere else; no other such body of nature literature as ours; no other people so close to nature in sympathy and understanding, because there is no other people of the same degree of culture living so close to the real, wild out-of-doors.

The extraordinary interest in the out-of-doors is not altogether a recent acquirement. We inherited it. Nature study is an American habit. What else had the pioneers and colonists to study but the out-of-doors? and what else was half as wonderful? They came from an old urban world into this new country world, where all was strange, unnamed, and unexplored. Their chief business was observing nature, not as dull savages, nor as children born to a dead familiarity with their surroundings, but as interested men and women, with a need and a desire to know. Their coming was the real beginning of our nature movement; their observing has developed into our nature study habit.

Our nature literature also began with them. There is scarcely a journal, a diary, or a set of letters of this early time in which we do not find that careful seeing, and often that imaginative interpretation, so characteristic of the present day. Even the modern animal romancer is represented among these early writers in John Josselyn and his delicious book, "New England's Rarities Discovered."

It was not until the time of Emerson and Bryant and Thoreau, however, that our interest in nature became general and grew into something deeper than mere curiosity. There had been naturalists such as Audubon (he was a poet, also), but they went off into the deep woods alone. They were after new facts, new species. Emerson and Bryant and Thoreau went into the woods, too, but not for facts, nor did they go far, and they invited us to go along. We went, because they got no farther than the back-pasture fence. It was not to the woods they took us, but to nature; not a-hunting after new species in the name of science, but for new inspirations, new estimates of life, new health for mind and spirit.

But we were slow to get as far even as their back-pasture fence, slow to find nature in the fields and woods. It was fifty years ago that Emerson tried to take us to nature; but fifty years ago, how few there were who could make sense out of his invitation, to say nothing of accepting it! And of Thoreau's first nature book, "A Week on the Concord and Merrimack Rivers," there were sold, in four years after publication, two hundred and twenty copies. But two hundred and twenty of such books at work in the mind of the country could leaven, in time, a big lump of it. And they did. The out-of-doors, our attitude toward it, and our literature about it have never been the same since.

Even yet, however, it is the few only who respond to Thoreau, Emerson, and Burroughs, who can find nature, as well as birds and trees, who can think and feel as well as wonder and look. Before we can think and feel we must get over our wondering, and we must get entirely used to looking. This we are slowly doing,—slowly, I say, for it is the monstrous, the marvelous, the unreal that most of us still go out into the wilderness for to see,—bears and wolves, foxes, eagles, orioles, salmon, mustangs, porcupines of extraordinary parts and powers.

There came to my desk, tied up with the same string, not long since, three nature books of a sort to make Thoreau turn over in his grave,—accounts of beasts and birds such as old Thetbaldus gave us in his "Physiologus," that pious and marvelous bestiary of the dark ages. These three volumes that I refer to are modern and about American animals, but they, too, might have been written during the dark ages. All three have the same solemn preface, declaring the absolute truth of the observations that follow (as if we might doubt?), and piously pointing out their high moral purpose; all three likewise start out with the same wonderful story,—an animal biography: one, of a slum cat, born in a cracker box. Among the kittens of the cracker box was an extraordinary kitten of "pronounced color," who survives and comes to glory. The next book tells the biography of a fox, born in a hole among the Canadian hills. Among the pups born in this hole was one extraordinary pup "more finely colored" than the others, who survives and comes to glory. The third book tells the biography of a wolf, born in a cave among the rocks, still farther north. Among the cubs born in this cave was one extraordinary cub, "larger than the others," who survives and, as is to be expected of a wolf, comes to more glory than the cracker-box kitten or the fox pup of the hills.

Such are the stories that are made into texts and readers for our public schools; such are the animals that go roaming through the woods of the American child's imagination. But no such kittens or cubs or pups lurk in my eight-acre woodlot. I have seen several (six, to be exact) fox pups, but never did I see this overworked, extraordinary, *cum laude* pup of the recent nature books.

So long as we continue to read and believe such accounts, just so long shall we find it impossible to go with Audubon and Thoreau and Burroughs, for they have no place to take us, nothing to show us when we arrive. Their real world does not exist.

But we know that a real, ordinary, yet a marvelous world does exist, and right at hand. The present great nature movement is an outgoing to discover it,—its trees, birds, flowers, its myriad forms. This is the meaning of the countless manuals, the "how-to-know" books, and the nature study of the public schools. And this desire to know Nature is the reasonable, natural preparation for the deeper insight that leads to communion with her,—a desire to be traced more directly to Agassiz, and the hosts of teachers he inspired, perhaps, than to the poet-essayists like Emerson and Thoreau and Burroughs.

Let us learn to see and name first. The inexperienced, the unknowing, the unthinking, cannot love. One must live until tired, and think until baffled, before he can know his need of Nature; and then he will not know how to approach her unless already acquainted. To expect anything more than curiosity and animal delight in a child is foolish, and the attempt to teach him anything more at first than to know the out-of-doors is equally foolish. Poets are born, but not until they are old.

But if one got no farther than his how-to-know book would lead him, he still would get into the fields,—the best place for him this side of heaven,—he would get ozone for his lungs, red blood, sound sleep, and health. As a nation, we had just begun to get away from the farm and out of touch with the soil. The nature movement is sending us back in time. A new wave of physical soundness is to roll in upon us as the result, accompanied with a newness of mind and of morals.

For, next to bodily health, the influence of the fields makes for the health of the spirit. It is easier to be good in a good body and an environment of largeness, beauty, and peace,— easier here than anywhere else to be sane, sincere, and "in little thyng have suffisaunce." If it means anything to think upon whatsoever things are good and lovely, then it means much to own a how-to-know book and to make use of it.

This is hardly more than a beginning, however, merely satisfying an instinct of the mind. It is good if done afield, even though such classifying of the out-of-doors is only scraping an acquaintance with nature. The best good, the deep healing, come when one, no longer a stranger, breaks away from his getting and spending, from his thinking with men, and camps under the open sky, where he knows without thinking, and worships without priest or chant or prayer.

The world's work must be done, and only a small part of it can be done in the woods and fields. The merchants may not all turn ploughmen and wood-choppers. Nor is it necessary. What we need to do, and are learning to do, is to go to nature for our rest and health and recreation.

IX

June

A REFERENCE to one of my notebooks shows that in June, 1895, there were thirty-six species of birds nesting within singing distance of my study windows; in 1907 there were thirty-two, the most distant nest being less than five minutes' walk from my door.

This is not a modern natural history story,—an extraordinary discovery that only I am capable of making. Start your own June list, and I warrant you will find as many. For there is nothing peculiarly birdy about my small farm. Any place as uncongenial to English sparrows and one that offers a fair chance to the native birds will keep you busy counting nests in June.

In the chimney built the swifts (three or four families of them); in the barn loft a small colony of barn swallows; and under the roof of the pig-pen a pair of phœbes, my earliest spring birds and often the latest with a brood.

A bushy hillside drops from the porch to the old orchard, and along this steep southern slope nested a pair of indigo buntings and a pair of rose-breasted grosbeaks (my rarest neighbors); also, here in the thick underbrush were found chewinks, thrashers, black and white warblers, song sparrows, and a pair of partridges.

In the orchard there were half a dozen chippies' nests, even more robins', two nests of bluebirds, and one each of the tree swallow, flicker, yellow warbler, chebec, downy woodpecker, kingbird, great crested flycatcher, redstart, and screech owl.

Baltimore orioles nested in the elms along the road; close to the little river were the nests of catbirds and red-winged blackbirds; a nest of swamp sparrows and of Maryland yellow-throats in the meadow, and in the woodlot a pewee's nest, a crow's nest, and three nests of ovenbirds.

All these I found; but besides these I know that a pair of yellow-billed cuckoos built somewhere near the house, as did a pair of blue jays, wood thrushes, and chestnut-sided warblers. These I am still waiting for. I need another June.

Not one of all these birds is rare or even shy, unless it be the swamp sparrow; none of them that the veriest beginner should not come to know in the course of one June. For these are almost domesticated, our near neighbors and friends, who desire and who will return our friendly, neighborly calls.

There are other birds, like the hawks, the owls, the herons, the rarer thrushes, sparrows, warblers, and marsh birds, that require time and tramping for their discovery. I know the very log in which I could find young turkey buzzards in June; the clump of dog-roses where a least bittern will build; the old gum that for years has harbored a pair of barred owls; the little cove where, spring after spring, a black duck nests. But I should need a vacation to visit these.

I watch the others between times,—between five o'clock in the morning and breakfast, between breakfast and train time and church time, and on Saturdays to and from the garden. If you are your own gardener, you can carry not only a hoe, but along with it a pair of field glasses. I even combine the care of my pig and the study of the phœbes that share his pen. Occasionally I drop everything and hunt for a nest, as if life depended upon my finding it. But life doesn't, the more's the pity, for me. Life depends on the finding of things that are very different from birds' nests, things that require a deal of hunting the whole year around. Yet I take the time to hunt birds' nests, too, for life is more than meat (I raise a good many vegetables), and, after all, *my* life does depend, in no small measure, upon my finding a few birds' nests in June.

I remember a June when I tried to get life out of a grocery store, and the sickness of it comes over me even yet at times. I sold kerosene oil, brown sugar, coffee, salt mackerel, and plug tobacco. I breathed the mingled breath of kerosene oil, brown sugar, coffee, salt mackerel, and plug tobacco,—the odor of mere money,—when I knew the fox grapes were in blossom, the magnolias and the azaleas; when I knew the fields were green and the birds were in song! I have longed for many things, but never as I longed that June for the farm, for the long, long day, yes, and for the long, long row. It was that kerosened, salt-mackereled, plug-tobaccoed—moneyed—June that took me back to sweet poverty and the farm.

I do not wish to think of living where the birds and wild flowers do not live with me. A city flat is convenient, and city life is exciting; but convenience and excitement plus meat and raiment are not the sum of life; neither, on the other hand, are pure air, sunshine, birds, flowers, a garden, quiet, and time to think, the whole of life. No; but when you consider the matter, there appears very little still needing to make life whole that you cannot have along with your birds, thoughts, and garden.

Whether you love the country or not, whether you know the difference between a kingbird and a kingcrab or not, you owe it to your body and your soul to get out into the open fields in June,—not to collect bird skins or birds' eggs or to make a herbarium or a nature diary, but to live a while where the birds and flowers live. The city may be heaven enough for you all the rest of the year; but God didn't make the city. There are seasons—March and February, usually—when it seems as if some one else has a hand in making the country. In June, however, the country is all and more than the poets say,—if it is poetry that you come out into the country for to feel.

Take my meadow, for instance, all aglow in June with buttercups, as if spread with a sheet of beaten gold! But now, if it is only hay that I am after (alas, too often it is), then my gold turns all to brass, and worse than brass, for buttercups, as my dairyman neighbor tells me, make the poorest kind of hay. I should keep no cow, perhaps. She gives nice milk, to be sure, but she eats up my beaten gold, she kills my buttercup poetry. Maybe I am too rich, I own too much: one cow, one horse, two pigs, thirty hens, fourteen acres of hills and trees. For it is the truth that I do not enjoy the foxes now as I did before I kept hens, nor the buttercups as I did before I got the cow. Suppose, now, besides all of this, I had money,—a lot of it!—several thousand dollars! You never get money along with a farm, and that is one reason why a farm is such a safe and sure investment for the soul. It is not the cow nor the chores, but money in or out of the bank, that robs life of its June.

Nor is owning *one* cow like having a dairy farm. The average man had better keep his money in the bank than invest in more than one cow. A single cow cannot eat all the gold out of one's meadow. I am still glad for the buttercups; and where the meadow passes into the upland, where the butter-cups give place to the daisies, my gold runs into silver; which means certainly that I am not making the farm pay, for on a paying farm a daisy—weed that it is, and not a native weed at that—is more like a spot of leprosy than of silver. Our daisies are not even those sung by the poets, I understand. What of it? A ten-acre field of them lies snow-white in my memory, fresh with the freshness of early June and the sweeter freshness of boyhood. And as for poetry, I have my own for them,—the poetry of boyhood, of Commencement days at the Institute, and of girls in white frocks.

There is no particular flower that means June to me as the hepatica means March, the arbutus April, the shad-bush May, and the red wood-lily July. I cannot think of single blossoms, or of here and there a spot of rare flowers, in June, but only of pastures drifted white, meadows purple-misted, and rolling hillsides billowy pink,—of laurel, forget-me-nots, daisies, viburnums, and buttercups. This is no time to bota-nize. Leave the collecting can at home, for one day at least, and wander forth, not to hunt, but to drift and float, or, if you run aground, to wade knee-deep in June. A botanist who is never poet misses as much in the out-of-doors as the poet who is never botanist.

If there were no other flower in the month but the white water-lily, June would still be June. "Who can contemplate it," exclaims Mr. Burroughs, "as it opens in the morning sun, and distills such perfume, such purity, such snow of petal, and such gold of anther, from the dark water and still darker ooze! How feminine it seems beside its coarser and more robust congeners, how shy, how pliant, how fine in texture and starlike in form!"

How the water-lily and spatter-dock can grow from the same mud is past understanding. One has every grace, the other none. But the dock can live in stagnant water, which perhaps is a sort of compensation.

And these two, for me, are always associated with magnolias,—*Magnolia glauca*,—and magnolias are associated with "old, forgotten, far-off things." Their absence from my swamps here is part of the price I pay for my transplanting to these New England fields.

If that were all, it were price enough. But think of June in New Jersey, with buzzards soaring, cardinals whistling, and turtle doves cooing; with swamps magnolia-scented, and woods astir with box-turtles, pine snakes, pine-tree lizards, and 'possums! Then think of June in Massachusetts with none of these,—at least in my neighborhood!

What then? I could scarcely strain the magnolia's breath from the mingling odors if it were here, for the common air I breathe is the breath of blossoming clover, wild grape, elder, blackberry, rose, and azalea. I must almost smell them by *families*. For here are six wild roses perfuming my air, five viburnums, six dogwoods (these last quite lacking in perfume, be it said), and wild blackberries that I have never dared to number. Who wants to number them? to spend his June with a "plant analysis," dissecting and keeping tally? It is enough now to be alive and out of doors among the flowers. Nor is it all of June to find thirty-six species of birds nesting within a radius of five hundred and fifty-five and one half feet from your *front* door. I do not cite these figures in order to startle, but to suggest, if I might, the joyous medley of life in June, its variety and abundance. You may not be able to name all the warblers; you have never yet made out which is which among the dogwoods and viburnums; the dogwood flowers are all four-pointed stars, while the viburnums are all five-pointed. But what of it,—four or five, dogwood or viburnum! Here they are, banked in soft, snowy fragrance along the margin of the pond. A tiny nest swings from a fork among them, a tiny bird with a white ring around her eye broods and watches you drift past. You have a fish-pole, and all about you and within you is the June.

X
A Broken Feather

ONE of the pair of crows that nest in my woodlot has been flying over all winter long with a gap in his right wing. Three at least of the large wing feathers are missing, and the result is a perceptible limp. The bird moves through the air with the list of a boat that has shifted or lost its ballast. Were he set upon in the air by a hawk, as might happen if he were smaller, the race would be short. He is plainly disabled by the loss of these three feathers, and has been for months. Just how and when the loss occurred I don't know. It is likely, however, that the feathers were shot away in June,—in corn-stealing time. Now for nearly a year he has been hobbling about on one whole and one half wing, trusting to luck to escape his enemies, until he can get three new feathers to take the places of these that are missing.

Well, why, in all this time, if these three feathers are so necessary, has he not gotten them? He might reply, "Which of you by taking thought can add as much as one cubit to your stature, to say nothing of three hairs to the top of your head?"

By taking time (which is a fine human phrase for giving Nature time), and with the right conditions, you may add the cubit. So the crow may get his feathers. It is not an affair between the crow and his feathers, nor between the crow and Nature. It is wholly Nature's affair with the crow's feathers, and so seriously does Nature take it, so careful is she, so systematic, so almost arbitrary about it, that the feathers of crows, like the hairs of our heads, can truly be said to be numbered.

Nothing could look more haphazard, certainly, than the way a hen's feathers seem to drop off at moulting time. The most forlorn, undone, abject creature about the farm is the half-moulted hen. There is one in the chicken yard now, so nearly naked that she really is ashamed of herself, and so miserably helpless that she squats in a corner all night, unable to reach the low poles of the roost. It is a critical experience with the hen, this moulting of her feathers, and were it not for the protection of the yard it might be a fatal experience. Nature seems to have no hand in the business at all; if she has, then what a mess she is making of it!

But pick up the hen, study the falling of the feathers carefully, and lo! here is law and order, system and sequence, as if every feather were a star, every quill a planet, and the old white hen the round sphere of the universe. You will put her down reverently, awfully, this hen that you took up with such compassion, and you will say, "Such knowledge is too wonderful for me."

So it is, for the moult means a great deal more than the mere renewal of feathers, just how much more no one seems to know. This much is plain, that once a year, usually after the nesting season, it seems a physical necessity for most birds to renew their plumage.

We get a new suit (some of us) because our old one wears out. That is the most apparent cause for the new annual suit of the birds. Yet with them, as with some of the favored of us humans, the feathers go out of fashion, and the change, the moult, is a mere matter of style.

But the annual moult, first of all, is Nature's wise provision for the safety and warmth of the bird. Feathers are not only covering, as our clothes, but also means of locomotion, and, hence, the bird's very means of life. A year of use leaves many of the feathers worn and broken, some of them through accident entirely lost (as with my crow), and while they might last for two years, or even longer, Nature has found it necessary to provide a new plumage as often as once a year, in order to keep the race of birds at its best.

But there are other reasons, at least there are advantages taken of the moult for other ends: such as the adaptation of the feathers to the varying temperatures of the seasons,— heavier in winter and lighter in summer; also the adaptation of the color of the plumage to the changing colors of the environment,—as the change from the dark summer color of the ptarmigan to its snow-white winter plumage to match the snows of its far northern home; then, and perhaps most interesting of all, is the advantage taken of the moult, for the adorning of the bird for the mating season. Indeed, Nature goes so far, in some cases, as to cause a special moult to meet the exigencies of the wedding,—as if fine feathers *do* make a fine bird. All this to meet the fancy of the bride! so, at least, the scientists tell us. Whether or not her fancy is the cause, it is a fact that among the birds it is the bridegroom who is adorned for his wife, and sometimes the fine feathers come by a special moult.

Not far from my house is a nest of black-crowned night herons, or "quawks." Preparatory to the mating of the pair there started from the crown of the male (and female, also, in this case,) two or three white, rounded plumes, which now hang eight inches in length, waving gracefully to his shoulders. They are the special glory of the wedding time; but soon after the nesting season is over they will drop out, not to come again until he goes a-wooing Mrs. Quawk once more. In the white American egret, and in the snowy egret, the plumes number about fifty, and occur upon the back close to the tail. They are straight in the American, recurved in the snowy, and make the famous "aigrette" plumes of the milliner. The birds are shot in their nuptial dress, and so great has been the heartless demand that both species, once very abundant, are now almost extinct.

Bobolink is another special case. He has two complete moults a year. Now, as I write, I hear him singing over the meadow,—a jet black, white, and cream-buff lover, most strikingly adorned. His wife, down in the grass, looks as little like him as a sparrow looks like a blackbird. After the breeding season he moults, changing color so completely that he and his wife and children all look alike, all like sparrows. They even lose their name now, flying south under the assumed name of "reedbirds."

Bobolink passes the winter in Brazil, and at the coming of spring, just before the long northward journey begins, he moults again; but you would hardly know it to look at him, for, strangely enough, he is not black and white, but still colored like a sparrow as he was in the fall. *Apparently* he is. Look at him more closely, however, and you will find the brownish yellow color is all caused by a veil of fine fringes hanging from the edges of the feathers. Underneath are the black and white and cream-buff. He starts northward, and by the time he reaches Massachusetts the fringe veil is worn off and the black and white bobolink appears. Specimens taken after their arrival here still show traces of the yellow veil.

Many birds do not have this spring moult at all, and with most of those that do, the great wing feathers are not then renewed as are bobolink's, but only at the annual moult after the nesting is done. In fact, the moulting of the remiges, or wing feathers, seems to be a *family* affair, the process differing with different families; for these are the bird's most important feathers, and their loss is so serious a matter that Nature has come to make the change according to the habits and needs of the birds.

With all birds the order is for the body feathers to begin to go first, then the wings, and last the tail. But the shedding of the wing feathers is a very slow and carefully regulated process. In the wild geese and other water birds the wing feathers drop out with the feathers of the body, and all go so simultaneously that the birds cannot fly. On land you could catch them with your hands, but they keep near or on the water and thus escape, though times have been when it was necessary to protect them from their human enemies at this season by special laws.

The necessity for the moult entails many risks, for it exposes the bird to peculiar dangers; yet no single bird is abandoned during this period, none left without a way of escape. The geese, as we have seen, moult most rapidly and hence are most helpless, but there are few of their enemies that they cannot avoid by keeping to the water and grassy marshes; the hawks, that hunt by wing, moult so slowly that they do not feel a loss of power; while such birds as the quail and grouse, that always depend in part for protection upon the blending of their colors with the colors of their environment, seem especially so protected during the moulting season. A grouse blotched with light patches, where the dark-tipped feathers have fallen away, may so melt into the mottled color scheme of its background as to escape the sharpest eye.

Such a rapid, wholesale moult as in the case of the geese would be fatal to land birds. Instead, their primaries, or large wing feathers, drop out one or two at a time and symmetrically from the two wings. Oftentimes it is the two inner primaries that go first, then the others following one at a time, the outermost last. This order varies, as in the kingfisher. In the snow bunting all but two of the old primaries are gone before any new ones have grown as large as the secondaries. In the hawks, again, birds that must use their wings and must have them always at their best, the moulting of the wing feathers is very slow, lasting nearly the whole year. The homing pigeon, another great flier, but not of the same kind as the hawks, begins about May to moult his wing feathers, losing the tenth primary first, a month later the ninth, then the others at intervals of from eight to fifteen days.

It is quite enough to make one pause, to make one even wonder, when he finds that this seemingly insignificant matter is taken so seriously by nature, and that even here there is that perfect adaptation of means to end. The gosling, to cite another instance, goes six weeks in down, then gets its first feathers, which it sheds in the fall. The young quail, on the other hand, is born with quills so far advanced that it is able to fly almost as soon as it is hatched. These are mature feathers; but the bird is still young and growing, and soon outgrows these first flight feathers, so that they are quickly lost and new ones come. This goes on till fall, several moults occurring the first summer to meet the increasing weight of the growing body.

Where there are peculiar uses made of the tail, as with the chimney swifts and woodpeckers, there is a peculiar order of moulting. In most birds the tail is a kind of balance or steering-gear, and not of equal importance with the wings. Nature, consequently, seems to have attached less importance to the feathers of the tail. They are not so firmly set, and they are hardly of the same quality or kind; for if a wing feather is once broken or lost, after the moult, it must go unmended until the annual moulting time comes round again; whereas, if a tail feather is lost through accident, it is made good, no matter when. How do you explain that? I know that old theory of the birds roosting with their tails out, and so, through generations of lost tails, those feathers now grow, expecting to be plucked by some enemy, and so have only a temporary hold. Perhaps.

The normal, natural way, of course, is to replace a lost feather with a new one as soon as possible; but in order to give extra strength to the wing feathers nature has found it necessary to check their frequent change, and so complete is the check that the annual moult is required to replace one of them. The Japanese have discovered the secret of this check, and are able by it to keep certain feathers in the tails of their cocks growing until they reach the enormous length of ten to twelve feet.

My crow, it seems, lost his three feathers just after his annual moult; the three broken shafts he carries still in his wing, and must continue to carry, as the stars must continue their courses. These three feathers must round out their cycle to the annual moult. The universe of worlds and feathers is a universe of law, of order, and of reason.

XI

High Moon

LAZILY sailing clouds, and between them, far away, the illimitable blue! And how blue! how cool! how far away! Never does the sky seem of so real azure, so fresh and new, but so mysteriously distant, as upon such a July day as this; and never does the earth seem so warm and near. I lie outstretched upon it as close as I ever lay upon my mother's breast. I feel the crisp moss beneath me, the creeping of the beetle under my shoulder, the heat of the gray stone against my side. I throw out my hands, push my fingers into the hot soil and feel them take root. Mother earth! The clouds sail on; the bending blue recedes; and—heaven? It matters not. Here are my brothers,—the beetle, the moss, the gray stone; and here I lie in the arms of the mother who bore me.

I have questions to ask—to-morrow; dreams to dream—to-morrow; things to do—to-morrow. To-day I am free in the fields; to-day I am brother to the beetle and the stone; I am neighbor

to this ancient white oak in whose shade I lie; I am child to
the earth. It is enough to be to-day.

How warm is this mother breast, even here, under the tree!
The sun is overhead. The summer is at its height. The flood-
tide of life has come. It is high noon of the year.

The drowsy silence of the full, hot noon lies deep across
the field. Stream and cattle and pasture-slope are quiet in
repose. The eyes of the earth are heavy. The air is asleep. Yet
the round shadow of my oak begins to shift. The cattle do
not move; the pasture still sleeps under the wide, white glare.
But already the noon is passing.

Of the four seasons summer is the shortest, and the one
we are least acquainted with. Summer is only a pause between
spring and autumn, only the hour of the year's noon. But the
hour is long enough were we able to stop, to lie down under
a tree for the hour, unwearied, wide-awake, and still.

We can be glad with the spring, sad with the autumn, eager
with the winter; but it is hard for us to go softly, to pause,
to be still, complete, sufficient, full with the full, sufficient
summer; to hang poised and expanded like the broad-winged
hawk yonder far up in the wide sky.

But the hawk is not still. The shadow of my oak begins to
lengthen. The hour is gone even while it comes, for wavering
softly down the languid air falls a yellow leaf from a slender
gray birch near by. I remember, too, that on my way through
the woodlot I frightened a small flock of robins from a pine;
and more than a week ago the swallows were gathering upon
the telegraph wires. It was springtime even yesterday; to-day
there are signs of autumn everywhere. Perhaps, after all, there
is no such time as summer,—no pause, no rest, no quiet in
the fields, no hour of noon.

Yet I get something out of the fields, these slumberous July days, that is neither of springtime nor of autumn, a ripening, mellowing, quieting something, that falls only when the leaves hang limp, when the earth warms in the shadows, when the wood-lily opens in the sun, and the whir of the cicada times the throbbing of the heat. And when that something falls, then I know it is summer.

This is a late July day, but its dawn was still of the springtime. At daybreak the birds were singing, fresh and full-throated as in May; then the sun burned through the mist and the chorus ceased. Now I do not hear even the chewink and the talkative vireo. Only the fiery notes of the scarlet tanager come to me through the dry white heat of the noon, and the resonant, reverberated song of the indigo bunting, a hot, metallic, quivering song, as out of a hot and copper sky.

There are nestlings still in the woods. This indigo bunting has eggs or young in the bushes up the hillside; the scarlet tanager but lately finished his nest in the tall oaks; I looked in upon some half-fledged cuckoos along the fence. But all of these are late. The year's young are upon the wing. A few of the spring's flowers are still opening. I noticed the bees upon some tardy raspberry blossoms; and yonder, amid the fixed shining colors of the wooded ridge, I see the top of a chestnut tree, misty and tender, with foamy white bloom. These are the last of the season. The July flowering of the chestnut always seems delayed and accidental. The season's fruit has set, is already ripening. Spring is gone; the sun is overhead; the red wood-lily is open. To-day is summer,—noon of the year.

High noon! and the hour strikes in the red wood-lily aflame in the old fields and in the low thick tangles of sweet-fern and blackberry that border the upland woods.

This is a flower of fire, the worshiper of the sun, the very heart of the summer. How impossible it would be to kindle a wood-lily on the cold, damp soil of April! It can be lighted only on this kiln-dried soil of July. This old hilly pasture is baking in the sun; the mouldy moss that creeps over its thin breast crackles and crumbles under my feet; the patches of sweet-fern that blotch it here and there crisp in the heat and fill the smothered air with a spicy breath; but the wood-lily opens wide and full, lifting its spotted lips to the Sun, for it loves his scorching kiss. See it glow! Should the withered thicket burst suddenly into a blaze it would be no wonder, so little would it take to fan these glowing petals into flame.

The marsh marigolds of May spread the meadows with a glow of warmth, yet that was but a gilded fire beside the wilting, withering heat of this midsummer lily. That early flush has gone. There is hardly a fleck of spring's freshness and delicacy on the fields, none of the tenderness of the bluets that touched everything in May, none even of the softness of the hardwood greens that lasted far into June. The colors are set now, dry and glistening, as if varnished over. The odors, too, have changed. They were moist and faint then,—the fragrance of the breath of things. Now they are strong, pungent, heavy,—the tried out smells of the sweat of things.

Life has grown lusty and lazy and rank. It stood no higher than the heads of the violets along my little river at the coming of June; to-day I cannot catch a glimpse of the water without breaking through a hedge of swamp milkweed, boneset, and peppermint. Here are turtle-head, joe-pye-weed, jewel-weed, the budding goldenrods, and the spreading, choking, rasping smartweed. The year is full grown. It is strong, rich, luxuriant.

And how erect and unblushing! The pointed spireas, the

sumacs, the thistles, this crowd along the river, this red wood-lily, even the tall swaying spray of meadow-rue! Slender, dainty, airy, the meadow-rue falls just short of grace and delicacy. It feels the season's pride of life. It is angled, rigid, rank. Were there the slightest bend to its branches, the merest suggestion of soul to the plant, then, from root to spreading panicles, there had been more grace, more misty, penciled delicacy wrought into the tall meadow-rue than into any flower-form of my summer.

But the suggestion of soul in the meadow-rue, as in the whole face of nature, is lost in flesh. It is the body, not the spirit, that is now present. She is well fed, well clothed, opulent, mature. She is conventional,—as conventional as a single, stiff spire of the steeple-bush,—turned to such a pointed nicety as to seem done by machine.

And yet the steeple-bush rarely grows as single spires, but by the meadow-full. We rarely see a single spire. We never gather summer flowers one by one, as we gather the arbutus and hepatica of spring. Life has lost its individuality. It is all massed, crowded, communal. The odors mingle now and drift wide on the winds, and as wide on the hillsides spread the colors, gold and green and white, and, where the rocky pasture runs down to the woods, the pink of the steeple-bush, like a flush of dawn.

Across my neighbor's pasture lies this soft glory of the spireas all through July. It runs in irregular streams down to the brook, rising there into a low-hanging bank of mist where the clustering spires of pink are interspersed with the taller, whiter meadow-sweet,—the "willow-leaved spirea."

There are shadowy rooms in the deep woods where the spring lingers until the leaves of autumn begin to fall. Here, in July, I can find the little twin flowers Linnea and Mitchella, blossoms that should have opened with the bloodroot and anemone. But Life has largely fled the woods and left them empty and still. She is out in the open, along the roadsides, rioting in the sun. The time of her maidenhood is gone. She is entirely maternal now, bent on replenishing the earth, on reseeding it against all possibility of death. She covers the ground with seed, and fills the very air with seed that the winds may sow. She has grown lusty, bold, almost defiant, no longer asking leave, but claiming for her own the pastures, gardens, waysides, even the dumps and waste places.

Yonder where the cattle feed stands the barbed purple thistle, arrogant, royal, unapproachable by man or beast. "Stand back," it says, by every one of its thousand nettles; "this field is mine." How savage and how splendid it is! After the royal purple fades, the goldfinches will dare to come and eat the plumed seeds and scatter them by the million, but even the goldfinch has been known to perish upon the poisoned spikes with which the plant is armed.

As persistent and successful as the thistle, though not as arrogant and savage, grows the wild white carrot in the mowing fields. The courts have called it names and set a price upon its life. It has been pulled out, cut off and burned,—exterminated again and again by statute.

Life snaps her fingers at us in July; lays hold of us, even, as we pass, and makes us carry her burs and beggar's-ticks for a wider planting. I am as useful as the tail of my cow. Neither the cow nor I ever come home from the July fields without an abundant sowing of stick-tights, tick-seeds, and burdock burs.

There is little beauty, fragrance, or even economic value in this wild, overrunning host of thistles, docks, daisies, plantains, yarrows, carrots, that now possess the earth; but when they crowd out along the dusty roadsides and cover the sterile, neglected, and unsightly places, we can sing, like the good gray poet, "the leaves and flowers of the commonest weeds" in our "Song of Joys."

There is certainly some praise due the chicory, or blue corn-flower, for it is a waste transformer, a "slummer" among flowers, if ever there was one. Like the daisy, it is a foreigner; but unlike the daisy, its coming is wholly benevolent. It asks only the roadsides, and for these along only the choked, deserted stretches; and where the summer dust lies deepest. Coarse, common, weedy, it doubtless is; but it never droops in the heat, and its blue shines through the smother like azure through the mists of the sky.

The winds and the birds are the sowers of the wayside, and to them I am indebted for this touch of midsummer color. But they miss certain spots along the roads, or else these are the patches that have no deepness of earth, where the seed of the winds' sowing can get no hold, for I have had to sow these myself. As I go up and down I carry a pocketful of sweet clover seed,—melilotus,—and over every waste and sandy place I scatter a few of the tiny seeds, when, lo! not two blades of grass where one grew before, but a patch of tall white flowers, breathing the sweetness of heaven into all the air, and humming in the July sun with the joyous sound of my honey bees. All this, and for season after season, where nothing grew before!

Along with melilotus in the gravelly cuts and burnt wood-lands grows the fireweed, a tall showy annual that waves its pink, plumed head throughout July. Farther north and west, this striking flower, like the melilotus, yields a heavy flow of delicious honey, but it does not attract the bees in this locality. Neither do my bees get any nectar from the fat little indigo-bush that takes possession of the unfarmed, sandy fields in July, though the wild bumblebees are busy upon it as long as it remains in bloom.

But this is not the native land of the honey bee, and it is sheer luck that the white clover, the basswood, the goldenrod, and here in July, the sumac, give down to these immigrant bees their honey-sweets.

High noon of the year! The laggard breeze comes to me now from the maple swamp, slow and sleepy with the odor of the white azaleas; a flock of chickadees stop and quiz me; the quivering click-clack of a distant mowing-machine fills the air with a drowsy hum.

Up to this time I have not seen a black snake, but now one is watching me with raised head from the edge of ferns among the rocks. One step toward him and the lifted, rigid neck, a flashing streak of jet, glides swiftly, evenly, mysteriously away, leaving me with an uncanny feeling of chill.

It, too, is a creature of the sun, as is everything that seems to belong especially to July. Smells, colors, sounds, shapes, are all sun-born. The hum of the insects, the music of the mower, the clear, strong hues of the flowers, the sweet breath of curing hay, the heavy balsamic odors of the woods,—everything seems either a distillation, a vibration, an essence, or some direct, immediate work of the sun.

Has your blood been work and winter faded until it runs thin? Would you feel the pulse of a new life? Come, we will take a day out of July and bask like the wood-lily and the snake; we will sleep for this one day in the blazing, sleeping, living, midsummer sun.

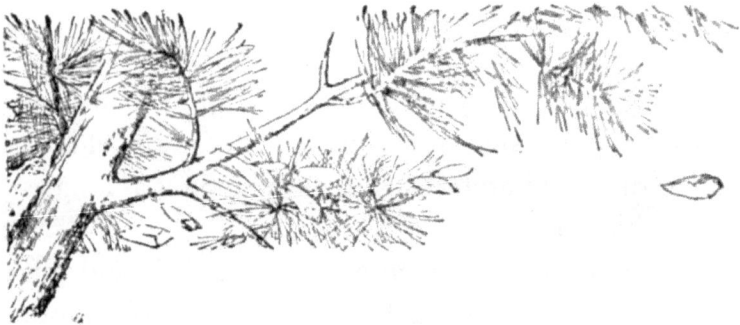

XII

The Palace in the Pig-pen

It is certainly a humble environment. The delicious spring of water, the plenty of wild, cool air, and the clean pavement of loose stones do not surround this home as they did the home of Mr. Burroughs's phœbes, nor does this look "out upon some wild scene and overhung by beetling crags." Instead, this phœbe's nest is stuck close up to the low board roof in my pig-pen.

"You have taken a handful of my wooded acres," says Nature, "and if you have not improved them, you at least have changed them greatly. But they are mine still. Be friendly now, go softly, and you shall have them all,—and I shall have them all, too. We will share them together."

And we do. Every part of the fourteen acres is mine, yielding some kind of food or fuel or shelter. And every foot, yes, every *foot*, is Nature's; as entirely hers as when the thick primeval forest stood here. The apple trees are hers as much as mine, and she has an average of ten different bird families, living in them every spring. A pair of crows and a pair of red-tailed hawks are nesting in the woodlot; there are at least three families of chipmunks in as many of my stone piles; a fine old tree toad (his fourth season now) sleeps on the porch under the climbing rose; a hornet's nest hangs in a corner of the eaves; a small colony of swifts thunder in the chimney; swallows twitter in the hayloft; a chipmunk and a half-tame gray squirrel feed in the barn; and—to bring an end to this bare beginning—under the roof of the pig-pen dwell this pair of phœbes.

To make a bird house of a pig-pen, to divide it between the pig and the bird—this is as far as Nature can go, and this is certainly enough to redeem the whole farm. For she has not sent an outcast or a scavenger to dwell in the pen, but a bird of character, however much he may lack in song or color. Phœbe does not make up well in a picture; neither does he perform well as a singer; there is little to him, in fact, but personality,—personality of a kind and quantity, sufficient to make the pig-pen a decent and respectable neighborhood.

Phœbe is altogether more than his surroundings. Every time I go to feed the pig, he lights upon a post near by and says to me: "It's what you are! Not what you do, but how you do it!"—with a launch into the air, a whirl, an unerring snap at a cabbage butterfly, and an easy drop to the post again, by way of illustration. "Not where you live, but how you live there; not the feathers you wear, but how you wear them,—it is what you are that counts!"

There is a difference between being a "character" and having one. "Jim" Crow is a character, largely because he has so little. That is why he is "Jim." My phœbe lives over the pig, but he has no nickname like the crow. I cannot feel familiar with a bird of his air and carriage, who faces the world so squarely, who settles upon a stake as if he owned it, who lives a prince in my pig-pen.

Look at him! How alert, able, free! Notice the limber drop

of his tail, the ready energy it suggests. By that one sign you would know the bird had force. He is afraid of nothing, not even the cold, and he migrates only because he is a flycatcher, and is thus compelled to. The earliest spring day, however, that you find the flies buzzing in the sun, look for phœbe. He is back. The first of my birds to return in the spring is he, often beating the bluebird and robin by almost a week. It was a fearful spring, the spring of 1904. How phœbe managed to exist those miserable March days is a mystery. He came directly to the pen, as he had come the year before, and his presence in that bleakest of Marches made it almost spring.

The same force and promptness are manifest in the domestic affairs of the bird. The first to arrive that spring, he was also the first to build and bring off a brood,—or, perhaps, *She* was. And the size of the brood—of the broods, for the second one is now a-wing, and there may yet be a third!

Phœbe appeared without his mate, and for nearly three weeks he hunted in the vicinity of the pen, calling the day long, and, toward the end of the second week, occasionally soaring into the air, flapping and pouring forth a small, ecstatic song that seemed fairly forced from him.

These aerial bursts meant just one thing: *she* was coming, was coming soon! Was she coming, or was he getting ready to go for her? Here he had been for nearly three weeks, his house-lot chosen, his mind at rest, his heart beating faster with every sunrise. It was as plain as day that he knew—was certain—just how and just when something lovely was going to happen. I wished I knew. I was half in love with her myself, half jealous of him, and I, too, watched for her.

But she was not for me. On the evening of April 14, he was alone as usual. The next morning a pair of phœbes flitted in and out of the windows of the pen. Here she was. Will some one tell me all about it? Had she just come along and fallen instantly in love with him and his fine pig-pen? There are foolish female birds; and there are records of just such love affairs; but this was too early in the season. It is pretty evident that he nested here last year. Was she his old mate, as Wilson believes? Did they keep together all through the autumn and winter, all the way from Massachusetts to Florida and back? Or was she a new bride, who had promised him before he left Florida? If so, then how did she know where to find him?

Here is a pretty story. But who will tell it to me?

What followed is a pretty story, too, had I a lover's pen with which to write it,—the story of his love, of their love, and of her love especially, which was last and best.

For several days after she came the weather continued raw and wet, so that nest-building was greatly delayed. The scar of an old, last year's nest still showed on a stringer, and I wondered if they had decided on this or some other site for the new nest. They had not made up their minds, for when they did start it was to make three beginnings.

Then I offered a suggestion. Out of a bit of stick, branching at right angles, I made a little bracket and tacked it up on one of the stringers, down near the lower end of the roof. It appealed to the birds at once, and from that moment the building went steadily on.

Saddled upon this bracket, as well as mortared to the stringer, the nest, when finished, was as safe as a castle. And how perfect a thing! Few nests, indeed, combine the solidity, the softness, and the exquisite curve of phoebe's.

In placing the bracket, I had carelessly nailed it under one of the cracks in the loose board roof. The nest was receiving its first linings when there came a long, hard rain that beat through the crack and soaked the little cradle. This was serious, for a great deal of mud had been worked into the thick foundation, and here, in the constant shade, the dampness would be long in drying out.

The builders saw the mistake, too, and with their great good sense immediately began to remedy it. They built the bottom up thicker, carried the wall over on a slant that brought the outermost point within the crack, then raised the whole nest until the cup was as round-rimmed and hollow as the mould of the bird's breast could make it.

The outside of the nest, its base, is broad and rough and shapeless enough; but nothing could be softer and lovelier than the inside, the cradle, and nothing drier, for the slanting walls shed every drop from the leaky crack.

Wet weather followed the heavy rain until long after the nest was finished. The whole structure was as damp and cold as a newly plastered house. It felt wet to my touch. Yet I noticed the birds were already brooding. Every night, and often during the day, I would see one of them in the nest, so deep in that only a head or a tail showed over the round rim. After several days I looked to see the eggs, but to my surprise found the nest empty. It had been robbed, I thought, yet by what creature I could not imagine. Then down cuddled one of the birds again,—and I understood. Instead of wet and cold, the nest to-day felt warm to my hand; it was dry almost to the bottom. It had changed color, too, all the upper part having turned a soft silver-gray. She (I am sure it was she) had not been brooding her eggs at all; she had been brooding her mother's thought of them; and for them had been nestling here these days and nights, drying and warming their damp cradle with the fire of her life and love.

In due time the eggs came,—five of them, white, spotless, and shapely. While the little hen was hatching them I gave my attention further to the cock.

I am writing this with a black suspicion overhanging him. But of that later. I hope it is unfounded, and I shall give him the benefit of the doubt. A man is innocent until proved guilty. I have no positive evidence of Mr. Phœbe's wrong.

Our intimate friendship has revealed a most pleasing nature in phœbe. Perhaps such close and continued association would show like qualities in every bird, even in the kingbird. But I fear only a woman, like Mrs. Olive Thorne Miller, could find them in him. Not much can be said of this flycatcher family, except that it is useful,—a kind of virtue that gets its chief reward in heaven. I am acquainted with only four of the other nine members,—great-crest, kingbird, pewee, and chebec,—and each of these has some redeeming attributes besides the habit of catching flies.

They are all good nest-builders, good parents, and brave, independent birds; but aside from phœbe and pewee—the latter in his small way the sweetest voice of the oak woods— the whole family is an odd lot, cross-grained, cross-looking, and about as musical as a family of ducks. A duck seems to know that he cannot sing. A flycatcher knows nothing of any shortcoming. He knows he can sing, and in time he will prove it. If desire and effort count for anything, he certainly must prove it in time. How long the family has already been training, no one knows. Everybody knows, however, the success each flycatcher of them has thus far attained. According to Mr. Chapman's authority, the five rarer members perform as follows: the olive-sided swoops from the tops of the tallest trees uttering "pu-pu" or "pu-pip"; the yellow-bellied sits upon the low twigs and sneezes a song, an abrupt "pse-ek," explosive and harsh, produced with a painful, convulsive jerk; the Acadian by the help of his tail says "spee" or "peet," now and then a loud "pee-e-yúk," meanwhile trembling violently; Trail's flycatcher jerks out his notes rapidly, doubling himself up and fairly vibrating with the explosive effort to sing "ee-zee-e-up"; the gray kingbird says a strong, simple "pitirri."

It would make a good minstrel show, doubtless, if the family would appear together. In chorus, surely, they would be far from a tuneful choir.

I should hate to hear the flycatchers all together. Yet individually, in the wide universal chorus of the out-of-doors, how much we should miss the kingbird's metallic twitter and the chebec's insistent call!

There was little excitement for phœbe during this period of incubation. He hunted in the neighborhood and occasionally called to his mate, contented enough perhaps, but certainly sometimes appearing tired. One rainy day he sat in the pig-pen window looking out at the gray wet world. He was humped and silent and meditative, his whole attitude speaking the extreme length of his day, the monotony of the drip, drip, drip from the eaves, and the sitting, the ceaseless sitting, of his brooding wife.

He might have hastened the time by catching a few flies for her or by taking her place on the nest, but I never saw him do it.

Things were livelier when the eggs hatched, for it required a good many flies a day to keep the five young ones growing. And how they grew! Like bread sponge in a pan, they began to rise, pushing the mother up so that she was forced to stand over them; then pushing her out until she could cling only to the side of the nest at night; then pushing her off altogether. By this time they were hanging to the outside themselves, covering the nest from sight, almost, until finally they spilled off upon their wings.

Out of the nest upon the air! Out of the pen and into a sweet, wide world of green and blue and golden light! I saw the second brood take their first flight, and it was thrilling.

The nest was placed back from and below the window, so that in leaving it the young would have to drop, then turn and fly up to get out. Below was the pig.

As they grew I began to fear that they might try their wings before this feat could be accomplished, and so fall to the pig below. But Nature, in this case, was careful of her pearls. Day after day they clung to the nest, even after they might have flown; and when they did go, it was with a sure and a long flight that carried them out and away to the tops of the neighboring trees.

They left the nest one at a time, and were met in the air by their mother, who darting to them, calling loudly, and, whirling about them, helped them as high and as far away as they could go.

I wish the simple record of these family affairs could be closed without one tragic entry. But that can rarely be of any family. Seven days after the first brood were a-wing, I found the new eggs in the nest. Soon after that the male bird disappeared. The second brood has now been out a week, and in all this time no sight or sound has been had of the father.

What happened? Was he killed? Caught by a cat or a hawk? It is possible; and this is an easy and kindly way to think of him. Nor is it impossible that he may have remained as leader and protector to the first brood, or (perish the thought!)

might he perhaps have grown weary at sight of the second lot of five eggs, of the long days and the neglect that they meant for him, and out of jealousy and fickleness wickedly deserted?

I hope it was death, a stainless, even ignominious death by one of my neighbor's dozen cats.

Death or desertion, it involved a second tragedy. Five such young ones at this time were too many for the mother. She fought nobly; no mother could have done more. All five were brought within a few days of flight; then, one day, I saw a little wing hanging listlessly over the side of the nest. I went closer. One had died. It had starved to death. There were none of the parasites in the nest that often kill these birds. It was a plain case of sacrifice,—by the mother, perhaps; by the other young, maybe,—one for the other four.

But she did well. Nine such young birds to her credit since April. Who shall measure her actual use to the world? How does she compare in value with the pig? Yesterday I saw several of her brood along the meadow fence hawking for flies. They were not far from my cabbage patch.

I hope that a pair of them returns to me another spring, and that they come early. Any bird that deigns to dwell under roof of mine commands my friendship; but no other bird takes phœbe's place in my affections, there is so much in him to like and he speaks for so much of the friendship of nature.

"Humble and inoffensive bird" he has been called by one of our leading ornithologies—because he comes to my pigpen! "Inoffensive"? this bird with the cabbage butterfly in his beak? The faint and damning praise! And "humble"? There is not a humble feather on his body. Humble to those who see the pen and not the bird. But to me—why, the bird has made a palace of my pig-pen.

The very pig seems less a pig because of this exquisite association; and the lowly work of feeding the creature has been
turned by phœbe into an æsthetic course in bird study.

XIII

An Account with Nature

THERE were chipmunks everywhere. The stone walls squeaked with them. At every turn, from early spring to early autumn, a chipmunk was scurrying away from you. Chipmunks were common. They did no particular harm, no particular good; they did nothing in particular, being only chipmunks and common, until one morning (it was June-bug time) I stopped and watched a chipmunk that sat atop the stone wall down in the orchard. He was eating, and the shells of his meal lay in a little pile upon the big flat stone which served as his table.

They were acorn shells, I thought, yet June seemed rather early in the season for acorns, and looking closer I discovered that the pile was entirely composed of June-bug shells,—wings and hollow bodies of the pestiferous beetles!

Well, well! I had never seen this before, never even heard of it. Chipmunk, a *useful* member of society! actually eating bugs in this bug-ridden world of mine! This was interesting and important. Why, I had really never known chipmunk, after all!

So I hadn't. He had always been too common. Flying squirrels were more worth while, because there were none on the farm. Now, however, I determined to cultivate the acquaintance of chipmunk, for there might be other discoveries awaiting me.

And there were. A narrow strip of grass separated the orchard and my garden patch. It was on my way to the garden that I most often stopped to watch this chipmunk, or rather the pair of them, in the orchard wall. June advanced, the beetles disappeared, and my garden grew apace. For the first time in four years there were prospects of good strawberries. Most of my small patch was given over to a new berry, one that I had originated, and I was waiting with an eagerness which was almost anxiety for the earliest berries.

The two chipmunks in the wall were now seven, the young ones quite as large as their parents, and both young and old on the best of terms with me.

I had put a little stick beside each of the three big berries that were reddening first (though I could have walked from the house blindfolded and picked them). I might have had the biggest of the three on June 7th, but for the sake of the flavor I thought it best to wait another day. On the 8th I went down with a box to get it. The big berry was gone, and so was one of the others, while only half of the third was left on the vine!

Gardening has its disappointments, its seasons of despair,— and wrath, too. Had a toad showed himself at that moment he would have fared badly. I snatched a stone and let it go at a robin flying over, for more than likely it was he who had stolen my berries. On the garden wall sat a friendly chipmunk eyeing me sympathetically.

Three days later several fine berries were ripe. On my way to the garden I passed the chipmunks in the orchard. A shining red spot among the vine-covered stones of their wall brought me to a stop, for I thought, on the instant, that it was my rose-breasted grosbeak, and that I was about to get a clue to its nest. Then up to the slab where he ate the June-bugs scrambled the chipmunk, and the rose-red spot on the breast of the grosbeak dissolved into a big scarlet-red strawberry. And by its long wedge shape I knew it was one of my new variety.

I hurried across to the patch and found every berry gone, while a line of bloody fragments led me back to the orchard wall, where a half dozen fresh calyx crowns completed my second discovery.

No, it did not complete it. It took a little watching to find out that the whole family—all seven!—were after berries. They were picking them half ripe, even, and actually storing them away, canning them down in the cavernous depths of the stone pile!

Alarmed? Yes, and I was wrathful, too. The taste for strawberries is innate, original; you can't be human without it. But joy in chipmunks is a cultivated liking, æsthetic in its nature. What chance in such a circumstance has the nature-lover with the human man? What shadow of doubt as to his choice between the chipmunks and the strawberries?

I had no gun then and no time to go over to my neighbor's to borrow his. So I stationed myself near by with a fistful of stones, and waited for the thieves to show themselves. I came so near to hitting one of them once that the sweat started all over me. After that there was no danger. I lost my nerve. The little scamps knew that war was declared, and they hid and dodged and sighted me so far off that even with a gun I should have been all summer killing the seven of them.

Meantime, a big rain and the warm June days were turning the berries red by the quart. They had more than caught up to the squirrels. I dropped my stones and picked. The squirrels picked, too, so did the toads and robins. Everybody picked. It was free for all. We picked them and ate them, jammed them and canned them. I almost carried some over to my neighbor, but took peas instead. You simply can't give your strawberries in New England to ordinary neighbors, who are not of your choosing. You have no fears at all as to what they will say to your peas.

The season closed on the Fourth of July, and our taste was not dim nor this natural love for strawberries abated; but all four of the small boys had the hives from over-indulgence, so bountifully did nature provide, so many did the seven chipmunks leave us!

Peace between me and the chipmunks had been signed before the strawberry season closed, and the pact still holds. Other things have occurred since to threaten it, however. Among them, an article in a recent number of a carefully edited out-of-door magazine, of wide circulation. Herein the chipmunk family was most roundly rated, in fact condemned to annihilation because of its wicked taste for birds' eggs and for young birds. Numerous photographs accompanied the article, showing the red squirrel with eggs in his mouth, but no such proof (even the red squirrel photographs I strongly believe were done from a *stuffed* squirrel) of chipmunk's guilt, though he was counted equally bad and, doubtless, will suffer with chickaree at the hands of those who took the article seriously.

I believe that is a great mistake. Indeed, I believe the whole article a deliberate falsehood, concocted in order to sell the fake photographs. Chipmunk is not an egg-sucker, else I should have found it out. But because I never caught him at it does not mean that no one else has. It does mean, however, that if chipmunk robs at all he does it so seldom as to call for no alarm nor for any retribution.

There is scarcely a day in the nesting season when I fail to see half a dozen chipmunks about the walls, yet I never noticed one even suspiciously near a bird's nest. In an apple tree, barely six jumps from the home of the family in the orchard wall, a brood of white-bellied swallows came to wing one spring; while robins, chippies, and red-eyed vireos—not to mention a cowbird, which I wish they had devoured—have also hatched and flown away from nests that these squirrels might easily have rifled.

It is not often that one comes upon even the red squirrel in the very act of robbing a nest. But the black snake, the glittering fiend! and the dear house cats! If I run across a dozen black snakes in the early summer, it is safe to say that six of them will be discovered by the cries of the birds they are robbing. Likewise the cats. No creature, however, larger than a June-bug was ever distressed by a chipmunk.

In a recent letter to me Mr. Burroughs says: "No, I never knew the chipmunk to suck or destroy eggs of any kind, and I have never heard of any well-authenticated instance of his doing so. The red squirrel is the sinner in this respect, and probably the gray squirrel also."

It will be difficult to find a true bill against him. Were the evidence all in, I believe that instead of a culprit we should find chipmunk a useful citizen. I reckon that the pile of June-bug bodies on the flat stone leaves me still in debt to him even after the strawberries have been credited. He may err occasionally, and may, on occasion, make a nuisance of himself,—but so do my four small boys, bless them! And, well—who doesn't?

When a family of chipmunks, which you have fed all summer on the veranda, take up their winter quarters inside the closed cabin, and chew up your quilts, hammocks, table-cloths, and whatever else there is of chewable properties, then they are anathema.

The litter and havoc that those squirrels made were dreadful. But instead of exterminating them root and branch, a big box was prepared the next summer and lined with tin, in which the linen was successfully wintered.

But how real was the loss, after all? Here is a rough log cabin on the side of Thorn Mountain. What sort of a table-cloth ought to be found in such a cabin, if not one that has been artistically chewed by chipmunks? Is it for fine linen that we take to the woods in summer? The chipmunks are well worth a tablecloth now and then,—well worth, besides these, all the strawberries and all the oats they can steal from my small patch.

Only it isn't stealing. Since I ceased throwing stones and began to watch the chipmunks carefully, I do not find their manner that of thieves in the least. They do not act as if they were taking what they have no right to. For who has told chipmunk to earn his oats in the sweat of his brow? No one. Instead he seems to understand that he is one of the innumerable factors ordained to make me sweat,—a good and wholesome experience for me so long as I get the necessary oats.

And I get them, in spite of the chipmunks, though I don't like to guess at how much they carried off,—anywhere, I should say, from a peck to a bushel, which they stored, as they tried to store the berries, somewhere in the big recesses of the stone wall.

All this, however, is beside the point. It isn't a case of oats and berries against June-bugs. You don't haggle with Nature after that fashion. The farm is not a marketplace where you get exactly what you pay for. You must spend on the farm all you have of time and strength and brains; but you must not expect merely your money's worth. Infinitely more than that, and oftentimes less. Farming is like virtue,—its own reward. It pays the man who loves it, no matter how short the oats and corn.

So it is with chipmunk. Perhaps his books don't balance,— a few June-bugs short on the credit side. What then? It isn't mere bugs and berries, as I have just suggested, but stone piles. What is the difference in value to me between a stone pile with and without a chipmunk in it. Just the difference, relatively speaking, between the house with or without my four boys in it.

Chipmunk, with his sleek, round form, his rich color and his stripes, is the daintiest, most beautiful of all our squirrels. He is one of the friendliest of my tenants, too, friendlier even than chickadee. The two are very much alike in spirit, but however tame and confiding chickadee may become, he is still a bird, and, despite his wings, belongs to a different and a lower order of beings. Chickadee is often curious about me; he can be coaxed to eat from my hand. Chipmunk is more than curious; he is interested; and it is not crumbs that he wants, but friendship. He can be coaxed to eat from my lips, sleep in my pocket, and even come to be stroked.

I have sometimes seen chickadee in winter when he seemed to come to me out of very need for living companionship. But in the flood-tide of summer life chipmunk will watch me from his stone pile and tag me along with every show of friendship.

The family in the orchard wall have grown very familiar.

They flatter me. I really believe, to be Emersonian, that I am
the great circumstance in this household. One of the number
is sure to be sitting upon the high flat slab to await my coming. He sits on the very edge of the crack, to be truthful, and
if I take a single step aside toward him he flips, and all there
is left of him is a little angry squeak from the depths of the
stones. If, however, I pass properly along, do not stop or make
any sudden motions, he sees me past, then usually follows me,
especially if I get well off and pause.

During a shower one day I halted under a large hickory
just beyond his den. He came running after me, so interested that he forgot to look to his footing, and just opposite
me slipped and bumped his nose hard against a stone,—so
hard that he sat up immediately and vigorously rubbed it.
Another time he followed me across to the garden and on to
the barbed-wire fence along the meadow. Here he climbed a
post and continued after me by way of the middle strand of
the wire, wriggling, twisting, even grabbing the barbs, in his
efforts to maintain his balance. He got midway between the
posts, when the sagging strand tripped him and he fell with
a splash into a shallow pool below.

Did the family in the orchard wall stay together as a family
for the first summer, I should like to know. As late as August
they all seemed to be in the wall, for in August I cut my oats,
and during this harvest they all worked together.

I mowed the oats as soon as they began to yellow, cocking
them to cure for hay. It was necessary to let them "make" for
six or seven days, and all this time the squirrels raced back and
forth between the cocks and the stone wall. They might have
hidden their gleanings in a dozen crannies nearer at hand; but
evidently they had a particular storehouse, near the home nest,

where the family could get at their provisions in bad weather without coming forth.

Had I removed the stones and dug out the nest, I should have found a tunnel leading into the ground for a few feet and opening into a chamber filled with a bulky grass nest,—a bed capable of holding half a dozen chipmunks, and adjoining this, by a short passageway, the storehouse of the oats.

How many trips they made between this crib and the oat patch, how many kernels they carried in their pouches at a trip, and how big a pile they had when all the grains were in,—these are more of the questions I should like to know.

I might have killed one of the squirrels and numbered the contents of his pouches, but my scientific zeal does not quite reach that pitch any more. The knowledge of just how many oat kernels a chipmunk can stuff into his left cheek (into *both* cheeks he can put twenty-nine kernels of corn) is really not worth the cost of his life. Of course some one has counted them,—just as some one has counted the hairs on the tail of the dog of the child of the wife of the Wild Man of Borneo, or at least seriously guessed at the number.

But this is thesis work for the doctors of philosophy, not a task for farmers and mere watchers in the woods. The chipmunks are in no danger because of my zeal for science; not that I am uninterested in the capacity of their cheeks in terms of oats, but that I am more interested in the whole squirrel, the whole family of squirrels.

When the first frosts come, the family—if they are still a family—seek the nest in the ground beneath the stone wall. But they do not go to sleep immediately. Their outer entrances have not yet been closed. There is still plenty of fresh air, and, of course, plenty of food,—acorns, chestnuts, hickory nuts, and oats. They doze quietly for a time and eat, pushing the empty shells and hulls into some side passage prepared beforehand to receive the débris.

But soon the frost is creeping down through the stones and earth overhead, the rains are filling the outer doorways and shutting off the supply of fresh air, and one day, though not sound sleepers, the family cuddles down and forgets to wake,—until the frost has begun to creep back toward the surface, and down through the softened soil is felt the thrill of the waking spring.

XIV

The Buzzard of the Bear Swamp

To most eyes, no doubt, the prospect would have seemed desolate, even forbidding. A single track of railroad lay under my feet, while down and away in front of me stretched the Bear Swamp, the largest, least-trod area of primeval swamp in southern New Jersey.

To me it was neither desolate nor forbidding, because I knew it well,—its gloomy depths, its silent streams, its hollow stumps, its trails, and its haunting mysteries. Yet I had never crossed its borders. I was born within its shadows, close enough to smell the magnolias of the margin, and had lived my first ten years only a little farther off; but not till now, after twice ten years of absence, had I stood here ready to enter and tread the paths where so long I had slipped to and fro as a shadow.

But what a pity ever to cross such a country! ever to map these unexplored child-lands to a scale of after years! I tramped the Bear Swamp over from edge to edge, letting the light of day into the deepest of its recesses, and found—a turkey buzzard's nest.

The silent streams, the stumps, the trails, I found, too, and there, it seems, they must be found a century hence; but the haunting mysteries of the great swamp fled away before me, and are gone forever. So much did I pay for my buzzard's nest.

The cost in time and trouble was what came near undoing my good uncle, with whom I was staying near the swamp. "What in thunderation!" he exclaimed, when I made known my desires. "From Boston to Haleyville to see a buzzard's nest!" As there are some things that even one's wife cannot quite understand, I didn't try to reason the matter of buzzards' nests with an uncle. If it had been a hawk's nest or a cardinal's, he would have thought nothing strange. But a buzzard's!

Perhaps my years of absence from the skies of the buzzard account for it. Yet it was never mere bird, mere buzzard, to me; so much more than buzzard, indeed, that I often wish it would sail into these empty New England skies. How eagerly I watch for it when homeward bound toward Jersey! The moment I cross the Delaware I begin to search the skies, and I know, for sure, when it swims into view, that I am near the blessed fields once more. No matter how wide and free, how full of clouds and color, my sky to the end will always need a soaring buzzard.

This is a burst of sentiment, truly, and doesn't explain at all why I should want to see the creature of these divine wings in the gruesome light of an earth-view, on its nesting stump or in its hollow log.

> Be Yarrow stream unseen, unknown!
>   It must, or we shall rue it:
> We have a vision of our own;
>   Ah! why should we undo it?

I understand. Nevertheless, I wanted to find a buzzard's nest,—the nest of the Bear Swamp buzzard; and here at last I stood; and yonder on the clouds, a mere mote in the distance, floated one of the birds. It was coming toward me over the wide reach of the swamp.

Its coming seemed perfectly natural, as the sight of the swamp seemed entirely familiar, though I had never looked upon it from this point before. Silent, inscrutable, and alien it lay, untouched by human hands except for this narrow braid of railroad binding its outer edges. Over it hung a quiet and reserve as real as twilight. Like a mask it was worn, and was slipped on, I know, at my approach. I could feel the silent spirit of the place drawing back away from me, though not to leave me quite alone. I should have at least a guide to lead me through the shadow land, for out of the lower living green towered a line of limbless stubs, their bleached bones gleaming white, or showing dark and gaunt against the horizon and marking for me a path far out across the swamp. Besides, here came the buzzard winding slowly down the clouds. Soon its spiral changed to a long pendulum swing, till just above the skeleton trees it wheeled, and bracing itself with its flapping wings, dropped heavily upon one of their headless trunks.

It had come leisurely, yet with a definiteness that was unmistakable and that was also meaningful. It had discovered me in the distance, and while still invisible to my eyes, had started down to perch upon that giant stub in order to watch me. Its eye had told it that I was not a workman upon the track, nor a traveler between stations. If there was a purpose to its movements that suggested just one thing to me, there was a lack of purpose in mine that meant many things to it. It was suspicious, and had come because somewhere beneath its perch lay a hollow log, the creature's den, holding the two eggs or young. A buzzard has some soul.

Marking the direction of the stub, and the probable distance, I waded into the deep underbrush, the buzzard for my guide, and for my quest the stump or hollow log that held the creature's nest.

The rank ferns and ropy vines swallowed me up, and shut out at times even the sight of the sky. Nothing could be seen of the buzzard. Half an hour's struggle left me climbing a pine-crested swell in the low bottom, and here I sighted the bird again. It had not moved.

I was now in the real swamp, the old uncut forest. It was a land of giants; huge tulip poplar and swamp white oak, so old that they had become solitary, their comrades having fallen one by one, or else, unable to loose the grip upon the soil that had widened and tightened through centuries, they had died standing. It was upon one of these that the buzzard sat humped.

Directly in my path stood an ancient swamp white oak, the greatest tree, I think, that I have ever seen. It was not the highest, nor the largest round, perhaps, but individually, spiritually, the greatest. Hoary, hollow, and broken-limbed, its huge bole seemed encircled with the centuries, and into its green and grizzled top all the winds of heaven had some time come.

One could worship in the presence of such a tree as easily as in the shadow of a vast cathedral.

> For it had bene an auncient tree,
> Sacred with many a mysteree.

Indeed, what is there built with hands that has the dignity, the majesty, the divinity of life? And what life was here! Life

whose beginnings lay so far back that I could no more reckon
the years than I could count the atoms it had builded into
this majestic form.

Looking down upon the oak from twice its height loomed
a tulip poplar, clean-bolled for thirty feet, and in the top all
green and gold with blossoms. It was a resplendent thing beside the oak, yet how unmistakably the gnarled old monarch
wore the crown. Its girth more than balanced the poplar's
greater height, and as for blossoms, Nature knows the beauty
of strength and inward majesty, and has pinned no bouton-
nière upon the oak.

My buzzard now was hardly more than half a mile away,
and plainly seen through the rifts in the lofty timbered roof
above me. As I was nearing the top of a large fallen pine that
lay in my course, I was startled by the *burrh! burrh! burrh!*
of three partridges taking flight just beyond, near the foot of
the tree. Their exploding seemed all the more real when three
little clouds of dust-smoke rose out of the low, wet bottom
and drifted up against the green.

Then I saw an interesting sight. In falling, the pine with
its wide-reaching, multitudinous roots had snatched at the
shallow, sandy bottom and torn out a giant fistful, leaving a
hole about two feet deep and more than a dozen feet wide.
The sand thus lifted into the air had gradually washed down
into a mound on each side of the butt, where it lay high and
dry above the level of the swamp. This the swamp birds had
turned into a great dust-bath. It was in constant use, surely,
for not a spear of grass had sprouted in it, and all over it were
pits and craters of various sizes, showing that not only the
partridges, but also the quails, and such small things as the
warblers, washed here,—though I can't recall ever having seen a

warbler bathe in the dust. A dry bath in the swamp was something of a luxury, evidently. I wonder if the buzzards used it?

I went forward cautiously now, and expectantly, for I was close enough to see the white beak and red wattled neck of my guide. It saw me, too, and began to twist its head as I shifted, and to twitch its wing tips nervously. Suddenly its long, black wings opened, and with a heavy lurch that left the stub rocking, it dropped and was soon soaring high up in the blue.

This was the right locality; now where should I find the nest? Apparently I was to have no further help from the old bird. The underbrush was so thick that I could see hardly farther than my nose. A half-rotten tree trunk lay near, the top end resting across the backs of several saplings which it had borne down in its fall. I crept up on this for a look around, and almost tumbled off at finding myself staring directly into the dark, cavernous hollow of an immense log lying on a slight rise of ground a few feet ahead of me.

It was a yawning hole, which at a glance I knew belonged to the buzzard. The log, a mere shell of a mighty white oak, had been girdled and felled with an axe, by coon hunters, probably, and still lay with one side resting upon the rim of the stump. As I stood looking, something white stirred vaguely in the hole and disappeared.

Leaping from my perch, I scrambled forward to the mouth of the hollow and was greeted with hisses from far back in the dark. Then came a thumping of bare feet, more hisses, and a sound of snapping beaks. I had found my buzzard's nest.

Hardly that, either, for there was not a feather, stick, or chip as evidence of a nest. The eggs had been laid upon the sloping cavern floor, and in the course of their incubation must have rolled clear down to the opposite end, where the opening was so narrow that the buzzard could not have brooded them until she had rolled them back. The wonder is that they ever hatched.

But they had, and what they hatched was another wonder. It was a right instinct which led the mother to seek the middle of the Bear Swamp and there hide her young in a hollow log. My sense of the fitness of things should have equaled hers, certainly, and I should have allowed her the privacy of the swamp. It was unfair of me and rude. Nature never intended a young buzzard for any eye but its mother's, and *she* hates the sight of it. Elsewhere I have told of a buzzard that devoured her eggs at the approach of an enemy, so delicately balanced are her unnamable appetites and her maternal affections!

The two freaks in the log must have been three weeks old, I should say, the larger weighing about four pounds. They were covered, as young owls are, with deep, snow-white down, out of which protruded their legs, long, black, scaly, snaky legs. They stood braced on these, their receding heads drawn back, their shoulders thrust forward, their bodies humped between the featherless wings like challenging tomcats.

In order to examine them, I crawled into the den;—not a difficult act, for the opening measured four feet and a half at the mouth. The air was musty inside, yet surprisingly free from odor. The floor was absolutely clean, but on the top and sides of the cavity was a thick coating of live mosquitoes, most of them gorged, hanging like a red-beaded tapestry over the walls.

I had taken pains that the flying buzzard should not see me enter, for I hoped she would descend to look after her young. But she would take no chances with herself. I sat near the mouth of the hollow, where I could catch the fresh breeze that pulled at the end, and where I had a view of a far-away bit of sky. Suddenly across this field of blue, as you have seen an infusorian scud across the field of your microscope, there swept a meteor of black,—the buzzard! and evidently in that instant of passage, at a distance certainly of half a mile, she spied me in the log.

I waited more than an hour longer, and when I tumbled out with a dozen kinds of cramps, the maternal creature was soaring serenely far up in the clear, cool sky.

XV

The Lay of the Land

SHE loved nature—from a veranda, a dog-cart, the deck of a vessel. She had been to the seashore for a whole June, the next June to the mountains, then a June to an inland farm. "And I enjoyed it!" she exclaimed; "the sky-blue, I mean, the sea-blue, and the green of the hills. But as for seeing fiddler crabs and chewinks and woodchucks—*things*! why, I simply didn't. In fact, I believe that most of your fiddling crabs and moralizing stumps and philosophizing woodchucks are simply the creatures of a disordered imagination."

I quite agreed as to the fiddling (some of it) and the philosophizing; I disagreed, however, as to the reality of the crabs and the woodchucks; for it was not the attributes and powers of these creatures that she really disbelieved in, but the very existence of the creatures themselves,—along *her* seashore, and upon the farm that *she* visited.

"As for fiddler crabs and chewinks and woodchucks—*things*," she did not see them. Certainly not. Yet a fiddler crab is as real an entity as a thousand-acre marsh,—and in its way as interesting. It is a sorry soul that looks for nothing out of doors but fiddler crabs, and insists upon their fiddling; that never sees the sky-blue, the sea-blue, and the green of the rolling hills. I shall never forget a moonrise over the Maurice River marshes that I witnessed one night in early June. It was a peculiarly solemn sight, and one of the profoundly beautiful experiences of my life, there in the wide, weird silence of the half sea-land, with the tide at flood. Nor shall I ever forget two or three of the stops which I made in the marshes that day to watch the fiddler crabs. Nor shall I forget how they fiddled. For fiddle they did, just as they used to years ago, when they and I lived on these marshes together.

If my skeptic found no fiddler crabs along her seashore, found nothing of interest smaller and more thing-like than color and fresh air, it may be that she did not understand how to look for crabs and things.

To go to the seashore for one June, to the mountains for a second, to the farm for a third, is not a good way to study the out-of-doors. A better way is to spend all three Junes at this shore or upon this same farm. It is when one abides upon the farm, indeed, the year around, through several Junes, that one discovers the woodchucks. The clover is too high in June. As one of twelve, June is a very good month to be out of doors; but as a season for nature study,—no single month, not even June, is satisfactory.

It takes time and patience and close watching to discover woodchucks. This means a limited territory; one can easily have too much ground to cultivate. I know a man who owns five hundred acres of Jersey pine barrens, and who can hardly till enough of it to pay taxes, whereas a friend of mine here near Boston is quietly getting rich on three acres and a half.

My skeptic had too many acres. She went to the seashore one summer, then to the mountains, then to a farm, and now she doubts the existence of crabs and woodchucks. Well she may. She might almost doubt the reality of the mountains and shore, to say nothing of the farm. One can scarcely come to believe in a mountain in the course of a mere June. The trouble is one of size. As well try to make friends with a crowded street. Crabs and woodchucks live in little holes. You must hunt for the holes; you must wait until the woodchucks come out.

For more than five years now I have been hunting holes here on the farm, and it is astonishing the number I have discovered. I doubt if driving past you would see anything extraordinary in this small farm of mine,—a steep, tree-grown ridge, with a house at the top, a patch of garden, a bit of meadow, a piece of woods, a stream, a few old apple trees, a rather sterile, stony field. But live here as I do, mow and dig and trim and chop as I do, know all the paths, the stumps, the stone heaps, the tree holes, earth holes,—there simply is no end of holes, and they are all inhabited.

By actual count there are forty-six woodchuck holes on these fourteen acres. Now forty-six woodchuck holes are a good many holes, but I have been these five years counting them. Only two of them are in the open, and visible from the road. Driving past, I say, you might actually think I had no woodchucks at all!

You should stop all summer and milk for me some morning. Throughout the early part of the season I had left the kitchen with my milk-pail rather late,—a little after five o'clock. One morning in September I stepped out of the door a little before five, and there in the clover close to the stoop sat a fine old woodchuck. I stood still and watched him. He was not expecting me yet, for he knew my comings out and goings in. He was up to his eyes in the clover, and he neither saw nor heard me.

Here about the kitchen door he had fed since the clover started, and I had not known it. He had timed his breakfast so as to be through by five o'clock,—before I came out. Had I been a boarder, with no cow to milk, perhaps I never should have known it. But after that morning I saw him frequently. I took pains to get up with him. Just over the edge of the lawn, about five feet down the wooded slope, was his burrow, which was one of the latest of the forty-six holes to be discovered.

When I shall have been milking and huckleberrying and hen's nesting and aimlessly wandering over these fourteen acres for five years more, I shall have found, it may be, the very last of the woodchuck holes. No, not in five, nor in five hundred years, for the families in the old holes keep multiplying, and the new holes keep multiplying too.

But woodchucks are not the only "things," not the only crop that the farm yields, although it must certainly seem that there can be little room on these scant acres for anything more. My farming, however, is intensive,—from the tops of my tallest pines to the bottoms of my deepest woodchuck burrows,—so that I have an abundant crop of crows, chipmunks, muskrats, mice, skunks, foxes, and rabbits (few rabbits, I ought to say, because of the many foxes).

Lately I found a den of young foxes within barking distance of the house, but along a stony ridge on the adjoining farm. No one would believe in the number of foxes (or the number of times I have counted the same fox) here on the farm, and this only sixteen miles by the roundabout road from Boston Common! But let him live here—and keep chickens!

One day, as we were sitting down to a noon dinner, I heard

the hens squawk, and out I tore. The fox had a big black hen and was making off for the woods. I made after the fox. There is a sharp ridge back of the henyard, which was thickly covered with stump sprouts and slashings. The fox took to the ridge. From the house to the henyard it is all downhill, and I wanted that hen. She weighed a good eight pounds,—a load for any fox,—and what with her squawking and flopping, the tangle of brush and the steep hillside, it is small wonder that just short of the top I fell upon her, to the great sorrow of the fox, who held on until I was within reach of him.

But such an experience as this, while it would be quite impossible to a summer boarder, is yet a not uncommon experience for my unobserving, fox-hating neighbors. They seldom see more, however; whereas, a study of the lay of the land hereabout reveals a real fox community overlying our farm community like some faint tracing. We humans possess the land by day and the foxes keep to their dens; the foxes possess the land at night and we humans take to our dens.

One of the high roads of the foxes runs across the farm. Foxes, like men, are more or less mechanical in their coming and going. They will move within certain well-defined boundaries, running certain definite routes; crossing the stream at a particular ford every time, traveling this ridge and not that, leaving the road at this point, and swinging off in just such a circle through the swamp.

One autumn two foxes were shot at my lower bars as they were jumping the little river. Their road crosses the stream here, then leads through the bars, along the base of the ridge, and up my path to the pasture.

I stood in this path one night when a fox that the dogs were driving came up behind me, stopped, and sniffed at my boots. This last November, 1907, a young fox, leaving the hounds in the tangle of his trails, trotted up this same path, turned in the pasture, and came up to the house. He halted on the edge of the lawn just above the woodchuck hole that I mentioned a few pages back, and for full ten minutes sat there in the moonlight yapping back at the shepherd dog barking at him from my neighbor's yard below.

This run up the ridge to the pasture is the highway from west to east. When the pack is baying off to the eastward, and coming nearer, I can stand by the fence between the yard and my neighbor's pasture with the certainty of seeing the fox once in half a dozen times, and the dogs almost every time, for the fox breaks from the sprout land back of the henyard, crosses the neighboring pasture, jumps the wall, and runs my driveway to the public road and on to the woods beyond the river.

All of this sounds very wild, indeed, and so it is—at night; in the daylight it is all tame enough. Only the patient watcher knows what wild feet run these open roads; only he who knows the lay of every foot of this rocky, pastured land knows that these winding cow paths lead past the barnyards on into the ledges and into dens. And no one can find all of this out in a single June.

Many of our happiest glimpses of nature are accidental. We stumble upon things, yet it happens usually when we are trying to find something. The finding of a hummingbird's nest is always an accident; and such accidents are extremely rare, as will be seen from a statement by Mr. Burroughs in which he says he has come upon but three hummingbirds' nests in all his life! He has doubtless found many more than three owls' nests, but perhaps not one of such finds was an accident. He *hunted* for the owls.

Night after night, in the sweet silence through which our little river sings, we hear the whimpering of the small screech owls. They are beating for mice and frogs over the meadow. So much we get without watching; but the sight of them and their nest, that came only with my visiting every tree in the neighborhood having a cavity big enough to hold the birds.

At twilight, in the late spring and early summer, we frequently hear a gentle, tremulous call from the woods, or from below in the orchard. "What is it?" I had been asked a hundred times, and as many times had answered that it sounded like the hen partridge clucking to her brood; or that it made me think of the mate-call of a coon; or that I half inclined to believe it the cry of the woodchucks; or that possibly it might be made by the owls. In fact, I didn't know the peculiar call, and year after year I kept waiting for an accident to reveal its maker and its meaning to me.

There were accidents and discoveries of many sorts during these years, but not this particular accident. The accident you wait for is slow in coming.

We were seated one evening on the porch listening to the whip-poor-wills, when some one said, "There's your woodchuck singing again." Sure enough, there sounded the tremulous woodchuck-partridge-coon-owl cry, and I slipped down through the birches determined to know that cry if I had to follow it all night.

The moon was high and full, the footing almost noiseless, and everything so quiet that I quickly located the clucking sounds as coming from the orchard. I came out of the birches into the wood road, and was crossing the open field to the orchard, when something dropped with a swish and a vicious clacking almost upon my head. I jumped from under,—I should say a part of my hair,—and saw a screech owl swoop softly up into the nearest apple tree. Instantly she turned toward me and uttered the gentle purring cluck that I had been guessing so hard at for at least three years. And even while I looked at her I saw in the tree beyond, silhouetted against the moonlit sky, two round bunches,—young owls evidently,—which were the interpretation of the calls. These two, and another young one, were found in the orchard the following day.

I rejoined the guessers on the porch, and gave them the satisfying facts. But let me say that this was very fast, even exceptional time, indeed, for the solving of an outdoor problem. I have questions enough for a big chapter upon which I have been *working* these more than three years. The point is this: I might have gone on guessing about the mother call of the screech owl to the end of time; whereas with a little searching and I must certainly have found out the cry in much less time than three years.

I had laughed at some good friends over on the other road who had bolted their front door and had gone out of the door at the side of the house for precisely twenty-one years because the key in the front door lock wouldn't work. They kept intending to have it fixed, but the children were little and kept them busy; then they grew up, and of course kept them busy; got married at last and left home,—all but one daughter. Still the locksmith was not called to fix the front door. One day this unmarried daughter, in a fit of dire impatience, got at the door herself, and found that the key had been inserted just twenty-one years before—upside down!

So I had sat on the porch and guessed about it. I had left the key upside down in the lock of the front door, and had gone out by way of the kitchen.

The first necessity for interesting nature study is an intimate acquaintance with some locality. It does not matter how small, how commonplace, how near the city,—the nearer the better, provided there are trees, water, fences, and some seclusion. If your own roof-tree stands in the midst of it all, then that is ideal.

But you must be limited. It is a small amount of land that one man can till with profit. Your very bees range hardly more than two miles from the hive. They cannot fly farther than that and store honey. Within this little world, however, they know every bank whereon the honey-yielding flowers grow. In early August I can follow their line of flight westward, through the woods for more than a mile, to an old pasture where great patches of dwarf sumac are in bloom. The bees hum about me in a fever of excitement. Then I fetch a compass far around toward home, and wherever I find the sumac in blossom, whether a hundred clustered bushes, or a single panicle of flowers hidden deep in the woods, there I find my golden bees. I wonder if, in all their range, they let waste one drop of this heavy golden sumac honey?

Do you know the flowers in your range as well as the bees know them in theirs? And, what is more, are you getting the honey? Do you know your dead trees and stone piles, and the folk who dwell in them? Could you take me, silent and soft of foot, from hole to hole, from nest to nest, from hedgerow to thicket, to cripple, to meadow, making me acquainted with your neighbors?

This is what Gilbert White could have done had you visited him at Selborne. This is what John Burroughs still does when the college girls go out to Slabsides.

Owning a farm is not necessary for all of this. Only the

parish house and the yard belonged to the old naturalist of Selborne. Sometimes, indeed, I am quite convinced that, for pure and lasting joy in the fields, you should not be possessed even of a garden patch; for, once you have digged into earth of your own, then have a care, else along with the cucumber seed you will plant your soul. The man in the Scriptures who bought a piece of land and wished thereafter only to dig, had a real case.

Owning a farm is not necessary. To be near the open country is enough, so near that you can know it intimately the year around. "He is a thoroughly good naturalist," says Kingsley, "who knows his own parish thoroughly." He was thinking of Gilbert White, I am sure,—that gentle rector who *lived* in Selborne, and there grew old with his tortoise.

This is all there is to nature study, this growing old with your garden and your tame tortoise. The study of the out-of-doors is not a new cult; it is not a search after a living uintatherium, or after a frog that can swallow his pond, or a fish hawk that reads,—not a hunt for the extraordinary or the marvelous at all, but for things as the Lord made them. Nature study is the out-of-door side of natural history, the unmeasured, unprinted side of poetry. It is joy in breathing the air of the fields; joy in seeing, hearing, living the life of the fields; joy in knowing and loving all that lives with you in *your* out-of-doors.